Kumon Math Workbooks

Grades P9-ECY-537

Are You Ready for High School Math?

Algebra

Table of Contents

KUMON

Fractions 1
Adding and Subtracting Fractions

Name

Date ___/___/___

Score ___/100

Remember It

Give these problems a try.

1. Find the GCF of the following number pair.

    (36, 63) → ☐

2. Find the LCM of the following number pair.

    (8, 12) → ☐

3. Find the LCD then calculate the answer to the problem.

    $\dfrac{2}{5} + \dfrac{2}{6} =$

Need a little help? Check out Review It before moving on.

⟨Ans.⟩ 1. 9   2. 24   3. 30, $\dfrac{22}{30} = \dfrac{11}{15}$

Review It

The numbers 1, 2, 4, and 8 are **factors** of 8. The factors that two or more integers have in common are called **common factors**. The largest factor that two integers have in common is called the **greatest common factor (GCF)**. You can simplify a fraction by dividing the numerator and denominator by the GCF.

Ex. Find the GCF of (36, 63) → ☐

   The factors of 36: 1, 2, **3**, 4, 6, **9**, 12, 18, and 36.
   The factors of 63: 1, **3**, 7, **9**, 21, and 63.

   The GCF of 36 and 63 is 9.

The multiples that two integers have in common are called **common multiples**. The smallest common multiple is called the **least common multiple (LCM)**.

Ex. Find the LCM of (8, 12) → ☐

   Multiples of 8: 8, 16, **24**, 32, 40, **48**, ...
   Multiples of 12: 12, **24**, 36, **48**, 60, 72, ...

   The LCM of 8 and 12 is 24.

Find the LCM of the denominators before adding or subtracting two or more fractions with different denominators. This is called the **least common denominator (LCD)**.

Ex. Find the LCD, then calculate the answer to the problem.

   $\dfrac{2}{5} + \dfrac{2}{6} =$ → Find the LCM: (5, 6)

   Multiples of 5: 5, 10, 15, 20, 25, **30**, ...
   Multiples of 6: 6, 12, 18, 24, **30**, 36, ...

   $\dfrac{2}{5} \times \dfrac{6}{6} + \dfrac{2}{6} \times \dfrac{5}{5} = \dfrac{12}{30} + \dfrac{10}{30}$ Multiply to get the same denominator.

   $= \dfrac{22}{30} = \dfrac{11}{15}$ Add the numerators.

 © Kumon Publishing Co., Ltd.

Practice It

1 | For each of the number pairs, find the GCF and the LCM.

5 points each

(1) (4, 18)   GCF: _____   LCM: _____

(2) (7, 11)   GCF: _____   LCM: _____

(3) (42, 14)   GCF: _____   LCM: _____

(4) (24, 16)   GCF: _____   LCM: _____

2 | Calculate the answer to each of the following questions.

10 points each

> The LCD will sometimes be one of the denominators in the problem.

(1) $\dfrac{3}{8} + \dfrac{1}{6} =$

(2) $\dfrac{7}{8} - \dfrac{1}{4} =$

> A fraction whose numerator is greater than the denominator is called an improper fraction. Always reduce and write your answers as proper fractions or mixed numbers.

(3) $\dfrac{5}{12} + \dfrac{7}{8} =$

(4) $2\dfrac{8}{9} - \dfrac{5}{6} =$

> You can borrow from the whole number if the numerator of a mixed number is not large enough.

(5) $8\dfrac{1}{5} - 5\dfrac{3}{4} =$

(6) $1\dfrac{3}{5} + \dfrac{1}{2} + 2\dfrac{3}{4} =$

(7) $9\dfrac{5}{6} - 5\dfrac{3}{4} - 2\dfrac{2}{3} =$

(8) $3\dfrac{1}{2} - 1\dfrac{2}{3} + 2\dfrac{3}{4} =$

2 Fractions 2
Multiplying and Dividing Fractions

Name _____

Date _____ / _____ / _____

Score _____ / 100

Remember It

Give these problems a try.

Calculate the answer of each of the following problems. Reduce as you multiply or divide.

1. $\dfrac{2}{15} \times \dfrac{5}{12} =$

2. $3\dfrac{3}{5} \times 1\dfrac{1}{9} =$

3. $3\dfrac{3}{5} \div 6 =$

Need a little help? Check out Review It before moving on.

⟨Ans.⟩ 1. $\dfrac{1}{18}$ 2. 4 3. $\dfrac{3}{5}$

Review It

Ex. $\dfrac{2}{15} \times \dfrac{5}{12} = \quad \rightarrow \quad \dfrac{2^{1}}{15^{3}} \times \dfrac{5^{1}}{12^{6}} = \dfrac{1}{18}$

When multiplying or dividing fractions, convert mixed numbers to improper fractions.

Ex. $3\dfrac{3}{5} \times 1\dfrac{1}{9} = \quad \rightarrow \quad 3\dfrac{3}{5} \times 1\dfrac{1}{9} = \dfrac{18^{2}}{5^{1}} \times \dfrac{10^{2}}{9^{1}} = 4$

To divide with fractions, flip the second fraction to get its **reciprocal**, then multiply.

Ex. $3\dfrac{3}{5} \div 6 = \quad \rightarrow \quad$ Changing 6 into an improper fraction, the problem becomes:

$$3\dfrac{3}{5} \div 6 = \dfrac{18}{5} \div \dfrac{6}{1}$$

$$\dfrac{18}{5} \div \dfrac{6}{1} = \dfrac{18^{3}}{5} \times \dfrac{1}{6^{1}} = \dfrac{3}{5}$$

 © *Kumon Publishing Co., Ltd.*

pp. 1–65
Algebra

pp. 67–151
Geometry

pp. 153–183
Probability & Statistics

pp. 185–197
Review

 Practice It

1 Calculate the answer of each of the following problems. Reduce as you multiply or divide.

10 points each

(1) $\dfrac{2}{3} \times \dfrac{4}{5} =$

(2) $\dfrac{4}{9} \times \dfrac{15}{16} =$

> Reducing as you multiply will make the problem easier! You won't have to reduce your answer.

(3) $2\dfrac{2}{7} \times \dfrac{3}{4} =$

(4) $4\dfrac{1}{2} \times 5\dfrac{2}{3} =$

(5) $\dfrac{5}{8} \div \dfrac{1}{2} =$

(6) $3\dfrac{1}{2} \div 6\dfrac{3}{4} =$

(7) $5\dfrac{1}{4} \times 1\dfrac{1}{13} \times 8\dfrac{2}{3} =$

(8) $3\dfrac{3}{5} \div \dfrac{2}{3} \times 5\dfrac{5}{6} =$

2 Answer each word problem by rewriting the question as an expression with fractions, and then calculate the expression.

10 points each

(1) Lilli walks $2\dfrac{1}{2}$ miles each day. How many miles does she walk after 6 days?

> Remember to include the units in your answer.

⟨**Ans.**⟩ _____ miles

(2) Baker John divides $\dfrac{2}{3}$ pound of flour between 2 cakes. How much flour goes into each cake?

⟨**Ans.**⟩ _____

Decimals and Percent

Name _____

Date _____ / _____ / _____   Score _____ / 100

Remember It

Give these problems a try.

> Don't forget to reduce any fractions in your answers!

1. Rewrite each decimal as a fraction.

0.35 Fraction: _____   3.2 Fraction: _____

2. Rewrite the percent as a decimal and a fraction.

30% Decimal: _____   Fraction: _____

3. Rewrite the fraction as a decimal and percent.

$\frac{2}{10}$ Decimal: _____   Percent: _____

Need a little help? Check out Review It before moving on.

⟨Ans.⟩ 1. $\frac{7}{20}$, $3\frac{1}{5}$ 2. 0.3, $\frac{3}{10}$ 3. 0.2, 20%

Review It

Numbers like 0.1, 0.5, and 2.3 are called **decimals**, and the "." is called the **decimal point**. The places to the right of the decimal point are called **tenths**, **hundredths**, **thousandths**, and so on.

$$0.2 = \frac{2}{10} = \frac{1}{5}$$
Tenths place

$$0.02 = \frac{2}{100} = \frac{1}{50}$$
Hundredths place

$$0.002 = \frac{2}{1000} = \frac{1}{500}$$
Thousandths place

Ex. Rewrite each decimal as a fraction.

$$0.35 \rightarrow \frac{35}{100} = \frac{7}{20}$$

$$3.2 \rightarrow 3\frac{2}{10} = 3\frac{1}{5} \text{ or } \frac{16}{5}$$

To change a percent into a decimal, move the decimal point two places to the left.

$$0.03 = \frac{3}{100} = 3\%$$
Hundredths place

$$0.30 = \frac{30}{100} = 30\%$$
Hundredths place

$$3.00 = \frac{300}{100} = 300\%$$
Hundredths place

Ex. Calculate the expression: $3\frac{5}{9} \times 0.6$

$$3\frac{5}{9} \times 0.6 = \frac{32}{9} \times 0.6$$

$$= \frac{32}{9^3} \times \frac{\cancel{3}^1}{5}$$

$$0.6 = \frac{6}{10} = \frac{3}{5}$$

$$= \frac{32}{15} = 2\frac{2}{15}$$

pp. 1–65
Algebra

pp. 67–151
Geometry

pp. 153–183
Probability & Statistics

pp. 185–197
Review

Practice It

1 Rewrite each decimal, fraction, or percent in terms of the other two.   10 points each

(1) 0.4   Fraction: _____   Percent: _____

> Move the decimal point two places to the right to quickly change a decimal to a percent.

(2) 70%   Decimal: _____   Fraction: _____

(3) $1\frac{2}{5}$ Decimal: _____   Percent: _____

2 Calculate each of the following problems.   15 points each

> Convert each decimal into a fraction first to calculate.

(1) $\frac{1}{5} + 0.4 =$

(2) $5.6 - 2\frac{1}{4} =$

> Reduce as you multiply.

(3) $0.375 \times \frac{5}{6} \times 3\frac{1}{5} =$

(4) $3\frac{1}{8} \div 1.5 \times 2\frac{1}{4} =$

3 Lisa has $7\frac{1}{2}$ pieces of paper. Each paper is 3.2 inches long. Lisa tapes the pieces of paper end-to-end to form one long piece of paper, and then cuts it into smaller pieces every 1.5 inches. How many pieces of paper will she have?   10 points

⟨Ans.⟩ _____

4 Exponents

Name _____

Date ____ / ____ / ____   Score ____ / 100

Remember It

Give these problems a try.

Calculate each of the following answers. Write your answer as mixed numbers, whenever applicable.

1. $2^5 =$

2. $\left(\dfrac{3}{4}\right)^2 =$

3. $\left(\dfrac{7}{11}\right)^0 =$

4. $\left(1\dfrac{1}{2}\right)^3 =$

5. $4^2 \times \left(\dfrac{1}{2}\right)^3 =$

6. $6^4 \div 2^4 =$

Need a little help? Check out Review It before moving on.

⟨Ans.⟩ 1. 32   2. $\dfrac{9}{16}$ 3. 1   4. $3\dfrac{3}{8}$ 5. 2   6. 81

Review It

Repeated multiplication can be shortened by using **exponents**. The number of times a **base** number is multiplied is given by the exponent.

Exponent Form	Read as...	Multiplication Form
2^2	two squared	2×2
2^3	two cubed	$2 \times 2 \times 2$
2^4	two to the fourth power	$2 \times 2 \times 2 \times 2$
2^5	two to the fifth power	$2 \times 2 \times 2 \times 2 \times 2$

Ex. $2^5 = \rightarrow$ The base, 2, is multiplied 5 times. $2^5 = 2 \times 2 \times 2 \times 2 \times 2 = 32$

A fraction can be a base. A numerator or denominator can also be a base on its own.

Ex. $\left(\dfrac{3}{4}\right)^2 = \dfrac{3}{4} \times \dfrac{3}{4} = \dfrac{9}{16}$ $\dfrac{3}{4^2} = \dfrac{3}{4 \times 4} = \dfrac{3}{16}$

Any number raised to the power of 0 equals 1.

Ex. $2^0 = 1$ $0.5^0 = 1$ $\left(\dfrac{7}{11}\right)^0 = 1$ $125^0 = 1$

Recall that we need to convert mixed numbers to improper fractions before finding a product. This is true for finding the product of an exponent expression.

Ex. $\left(1\dfrac{1}{2}\right)^3 = \rightarrow \left(1\dfrac{1}{2}\right)^3 = \left(\dfrac{3}{2}\right)^3 = \dfrac{3}{2} \times \dfrac{3}{2} \times \dfrac{3}{2} = \dfrac{27}{8} = 3\dfrac{3}{8}$

Ex. $4^2 \times \left(\dfrac{1}{2}\right)^3 = \rightarrow 4^2 \times \left(\dfrac{1}{2}\right)^3 = \overset{1}{\cancel{4}} \times \overset{2}{\cancel{4}} \times \dfrac{1}{\cancel{2}^1} \times \dfrac{1}{\cancel{2}^1} \times \dfrac{1}{\cancel{2}^1} = 2$

> When multiplying exponents with the same base, add the exponents. $2^4 \times 2^1 = 2^{4+1} = 2^5 = 32$
>
> When dividing exponents with the same base, subtract the exponents. $2^4 \div 2^1 = 2^{4-1} = 2^3 = 8$

When dividing numbers with the same exponents, simplify whenever possible. In division, you can simplify only when the exponents are the same.

Ex. $6^4 \div 2^4 = \left(\dfrac{\overset{3}{\cancel{6}}}{\underset{1}{\cancel{2}}}\right)^4 = 3^4 = 81$

 © Kumon Publishing Co., Ltd.

Practice It

1 **Calculate each of the following answers. Write your answer as mixed numbers, whenever applicable.**

10 points for (1)–(4), 15 points for (5)–(8)

(1) $3^4 =$

(2) $\left(\dfrac{2}{3}\right)^3 =$

> Convert mixed numbers to improper fractions before calculating.

> Remember that any number raised to the power of 0 equals 1.

(3) $\left(2\dfrac{1}{3}\right)^2 =$

(4) $\dfrac{3}{4^0} =$

(5) $8^3 \times \left(\dfrac{1}{2}\right)^5 =$

(6) $\left(2\dfrac{2}{5}\right)^2 \times \left(1\dfrac{2}{3}\right)^4 =$

(7) $\left(\dfrac{2}{3}\right)^4 \times \dfrac{5^0}{6^2} \times \left(4\dfrac{1}{2}\right)^3$

$=$

(8) $\dfrac{3^2}{4^3} \times \left(\dfrac{2}{3}\right)^4 \times \left(1\dfrac{1}{2}\right)^3 \times 2^5 \times \left(\dfrac{1}{3}\right)^2$

$=$

1 **Calculate the answer to each of the following questions.**   6 points each

(1) $1\frac{2}{3} + 3\frac{3}{4} + \frac{3}{8} =$

(2) $5\frac{1}{4} - 1\frac{2}{9} - 2\frac{1}{6} =$

(3) $\frac{2}{3} + \frac{4}{5} - \frac{5}{6} =$

(4) $12\frac{5}{7} - 6\frac{1}{2} + \frac{1}{4} =$

(5) $6\frac{2}{5} \times 3\frac{3}{4} =$

(6) $1\frac{2}{7} \div \frac{9}{28} =$

(7) $\frac{8}{9} \times 2\frac{1}{4} \div \frac{3}{5} =$

(8) $2\frac{7}{24} \times 6\frac{3}{8} \div 3\frac{2}{3} =$

(9) $\frac{3}{4} \div \frac{625}{1000} \times 4\frac{1}{6} =$

(10) $22 \div 1\frac{1}{13} \div 3\frac{1}{7} =$

2 Calculate the answer to each of the following questions.

6 points each

(1) $8^2 \times \left(2\frac{1}{4}\right)^2 =$

(2) $\left(1\frac{2}{3}\right)^2 \times 6^2 =$

(3) $\left(\frac{3}{4}\right)^4 \times \left(2\frac{2}{3}\right)^3 =$

(4) $\frac{4^2}{15} \times \left(1\frac{2}{3}\right)^3 \times \left(\frac{3}{5}\right)^2 =$

3 Answer each of the following word problems.

8 points each

(1) During a rinse cycle, $4\frac{2}{3}$ gallons of water flow into a washing machine every 2 minutes. How much water flows into the machine each minute?

(a) $2\frac{1}{2}$ gallons

(b) $2\frac{1}{3}$ gallons

(c) $7\frac{1}{3}$ gallons

(d) $9\frac{1}{3}$ gallons

(e) $14\frac{1}{3}$ gallons

(2) Sammi currently has 3.6 cups of white sugar in a container. She pours $\frac{2}{3}$ of the container into a pot to use in a recipe. Sammi then pours another $1\frac{1}{2}$ cups of brown sugar into the pot. How much total sugar is in the pot?

(a) 1.5 cups

(b) 2.4 cups

(c) 3.6 cups

(d) 3.9 cups

(e) 6.0 cups

Order of Operations 1

Name

Date   /   /

Score   / 100

Remember It

Give these problems a try.

Calculate the answer for each of the following problems.

1. $28 - 12 + 8 \div 4 \times 2 =$
2. $(6 - 2) + 4 - (24 \div 6) \times 2 =$

Need a little help? Check out Review It before moving on.

⟨Ans.⟩ 1. 20   2. 0

Review It

According to the order of operations,

- calculate the numbers in *parentheses* and *exponents* first,
- perform *multiplication* and *division* before *addition* and *subtraction*,
- then calculate from left to right.

Ex. $28 - 12 + 8 \div 4 \times 2 = 28 - 12 + 2 \times 2$ Multiply and divide from left to right.

$\qquad\qquad\qquad\qquad = 28 - 12 + \quad 4$ Add and subtract from left to right.

$\qquad\qquad\qquad\qquad = \quad 16 \quad + \quad 4$

$28 - 12 + 8 \div 4 \times 2 = 20$

Ex. $(6 - 2) + 4 - (24 \div 6) \times 2 = (4) + 4 - (4) \times 2$ Calculate within parentheses.

$\qquad\qquad\qquad\qquad\qquad = (4) + 4 - \quad 8$ Multiply and divide from left to right.

$\qquad\qquad\qquad\qquad\qquad = \quad 8 \quad - \quad 8$ Add and subtract from left to right.

$(6 - 2) + 4 - (24 \div 6) \times 2 = 0$

Practice It

1 **Calculate the answer for each of the following problems.**

10 points each

(1) $24 \div 4 \times 2 =$

(2) $24 - 16 \div 8 \times 2 =$

(3) $(18-3) - 2^3 + 6$

$=$

(4) $1\frac{1}{2} \times \frac{3}{4} \div \frac{2}{5} \times 1\frac{3}{5}$

$=$

(5) $10 - (3^2 - 2^3) - 2 \times 3$

$=$

(6) $5^2 \times 2 - 36 \div 2 \times \left(1\frac{1}{3}\right)^3 \div \left(2\frac{2}{3}\right)^2$

$=$

(7) $(8-2) + 12 \div 2 \times (0.5)^2 - 1 + 4$

$=$

(8) $(1.6)^2 - \frac{1}{2} \div (12 \div 3) \times 2 - \left(1\frac{1}{2}\right)^2$

$=$

2 Jill invents a new toy. She creates 5 copies in her office. She asks the factory to produce 4^3 copies. She then inspects the factory's copies and throws away 16 copies because of defects and approves the rest. Jill asks the factory to double the amount of toys that she has approved. Then she adds this amount to the original amount in her office. How many total toys does Jill have?

20 points

⟨Ans.⟩

Name _____

Date _____ / _____ / _____   Score _____ / 100

Remember It

Give these problems a try.

Calculate the answer for each of the following problems.

1. $\left(3\frac{1}{3}\right)^2 - 4\frac{1}{2} \times \left(3 - 1\frac{2}{3}\right)^2 =$

2. $9\frac{1}{3} - [(12 - 2^3) + 1] =$

Need a little help? Check out Review It before moving on.

⟨Ans.⟩ 1. $3\frac{1}{9}$ 2. $4\frac{1}{3}$

Review It

According to the order of operations:
- calculate exponents and numbers in *parentheses* and *brackets*, [ ], first (start with the innermost and continue to the outermost),
- perform *multiplication* and *division* before *addition* and *subtraction*,
- then calculate from left to right.

Ex. $\left(3\frac{1}{3}\right)^2 - 4\frac{1}{2} \times \left(3 - 1\frac{2}{3}\right)^2 = \left(\frac{10}{3}\right)^2 - \frac{9}{2} \times \left(\frac{4}{3}\right)^2$ Convert to improper fractions.

$= \left(\frac{100}{9}\right) - \frac{9}{2} \times \left(\frac{16}{9}\right)$ Calculate exponents and parentheses.

$= \left(\frac{100}{9}\right) - \frac{16}{2}$ Multiply and divide from left to right. Reduce as you go.

$= \left(11\frac{1}{9}\right) - 8$ Add and subtract from left to right.

$\left(3\frac{1}{3}\right)^2 - 4\frac{1}{2} \times \left(3 - 1\frac{2}{3}\right)^2 = 3\frac{1}{9}$

Ex. $9\frac{1}{3} - [(12 - 2^3) + 1] = 9\frac{1}{3} - [(12 - 8) + 1]$ Calculate exponents, parentheses, and brackets.

$= 9\frac{1}{3} - 5$ Add and subtract from left to right.

$9\frac{1}{3} - [(12 - 2^3) + 1] = 4\frac{1}{3}$

pp. 1–65
Algebra

pp. 67–151
Geometry

pp. 153–183
Probability & Statistics

pp. 185–197
Review

Practice It

1 **Calculate the answer for each of the following problems.** 12 points each

Calculate from inside to outside and left to right.

(1) $2^6 - 2^3 \times (8 - 2) \div 2$

=

(2) $[20 \div (2 + 3) - 2] \times 4$

=

(3) $10 \div 5 \times [20 \div (2 + 3) \times 4]$

=

(4) $35 - \left(6 \times \frac{1}{2}\right)^4 \div (11 - 9 + 1)^3$

=

Convert decimals to fractions whenever necessary.

(5) $(7 \div 3)^2 - 2\frac{1}{4} \div (0.75)^3$

=

(6) $(10 \div 2^2)^3 - \left(1.2 \times 1\frac{1}{4}\right)^2$

=

2 **Answer each of the following word problems.** 14 points each

(1) It takes Lisa 2.5 hours to build a birdhouse, and it takes her 0.25 hours to paint each birdhouse. Lisa builds and paints a total of 8 birdhouses. How much time does it take her?

⟨**Ans.**⟩ _____

(2) Each cake that Grant bakes weighs a total of 0.8 pounds. Grant bakes 3 cakes. He then places all the cakes in a display case that weighs $1\frac{1}{2}$ pounds. He repeats this entire process 4 times. What is the total weight of all of these items?

⟨**Ans.**⟩ _____

Name _____

Date ___/___/___   Score ___/100

Remember It

Give these problems a try.

Calculate the answer for each of the following problems.

1. $6 + (-2) =$

2. $-7 - (-4) =$

3. $(-2) \times \left(-\dfrac{1}{4}\right) \times (-10) =$

4. $\left(-6\dfrac{2}{3}\right) \div \left(-\dfrac{4}{9}\right) \times \dfrac{1}{2} =$

Need a little help? Check out Review It before moving on.

(Ans.) 1. 4   2. −3   3. −5   4. $7\dfrac{1}{2}$

Review It

Numbers greater than 0, such as 1, 2, and 10 are called **positive numbers**. Numbers less than 0 are called **negative numbers** and have a negative sign (−) before them, such as −1, −2, −3.5, and −4. −1 is read as "negative one." The number 0 is a special number and is neither positive nor negative.

A problem that involves adding a positive number (+) and a negative number (−) can be treated as a subtraction problem. Subtracting by a negative number can be treated as an addition problem.

Addition Examples	Subtraction Examples
$5 + (-3) = 5 - 3 = 2$	$3 - (-4) = 3 + 4 = 7$
$-1 + (-7) = -1 - 7 = -8$	$-5 - (-1) = -5 + 1 = -4$
$6 + (-2) = 6 - 2 = 4$	$-7 - (-4) = -7 + 4 = -3$

When multiplying or dividing negative numbers, count the number of negative signs.
• If there is an even number of negative signs, the answer is positive.
• If there is an odd number of negative signs, the answer is negative.

After determining if the answer is positive or negative, multiply the numbers to find the answer.

Multiplication Examples	Division Examples
$2 \times (-1) \times 3 \times (-5) = (2 \times 1 \times 3 \times 5) = 30$	$6 \div (-3) = -2$
$3 \times (-2) \times (-1) \times (-2) = -(3 \times 2 \times 1 \times 2)$	$-24 \div 4 \div (-2) = 24 \div 4 \div 2 = 3$
$\qquad\qquad = -12$	$\left(-6\dfrac{2}{3}\right) \div \left(-\dfrac{4}{9}\right) \times \dfrac{1}{2} = \dfrac{20}{3} \times \dfrac{9}{4} \times \dfrac{1}{2} = 7\dfrac{1}{2}$
$(-2) \times \left(-\dfrac{1}{4}\right) \times (-10) = -5$	

If you find these problems difficult, refer to a number line.

Both positive and negative numbers may be graphed on a number line.

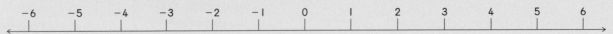

Practice It

1 Calculate the answer for each of the following problems by using addition or subtraction.

10 points each

> (−10) is the same as −10.

(1) $6+(-10) =$

(2) $7-(-15) =$

(3) $-3\dfrac{1}{4}-\left(-1\dfrac{1}{3}\right) =$

(4) $-\dfrac{5}{6}+\left(-3\dfrac{1}{4}\right) =$

2 Calculate the answer for each of the following problems by using multiplication or division.

15 points each

> If no order of operation rule applies, calculate from left to right.

(1) $(-3) \times 2 \times (-1)$

$=$

(2) $(-1) \times 2 \times 3 \times (-4) \times (-5)$

$=$

(3) $0.6 \div \dfrac{3}{4} \times (-8)$

$=$

(4) $\left(-3\dfrac{1}{3}\right) \div \left(-1\dfrac{1}{5}\right) \times (-0.7) \times \left(-4\dfrac{1}{2}\right)$

$=$

Negative Numbers 2

Name

Date / /

Score / 100

Remember It

Give these problems a try.

Calculate the answer for each of the following problems.

1. $\dfrac{\frac{3}{4}}{5-\frac{1}{2}} =$

2. $(-2)^3(-5) - (-12) \div 3 =$

Need a little help? Check out Review It before moving on.

⟨Ans.⟩ 1. $\frac{1}{6}$ 2. 44

Review It

If there is an operation in the numerator or denominator of a fraction, place parentheses around it to calculate the correct order of operations. Remember, fractions represent division.

Ex. $\dfrac{\frac{3}{4}}{5-\frac{1}{2}} =$ → Since $\frac{3}{4}$ is in the numerator and $\left(5-\frac{1}{2}\right)$ is in the denominator, we can rewrite the problem

by using the division symbol: $\dfrac{\frac{3}{4}}{5-\frac{1}{2}} = \frac{3}{4} \div \left(5-\frac{1}{2}\right) = \frac{3}{4} \div 4\frac{1}{2} = \frac{3}{4} \div \frac{9}{2} = \frac{\cancel{3}^1}{\cancel{4}_2} \times \frac{\cancel{2}^1}{\cancel{9}_3} = \frac{1}{6}$

When calculating exponents with negative bases, use the exponent to determine the number of negative signs in the equivalent multiplication problem.

• even power → positive product
• odd power → negative product

Note the differences in the examples below.

$4^2 = 4 \times 4 = 16$

$-4^2 = -(4^2) = -(4 \times 4) = -16$

$(-4)^2 = (-4) \times (-4) = 16$

$-(-4)^2 = -[(-4) \times (-4)] = -16$

$4^3 = 4 \times 4 \times 4 = 64$

$-4^3 = -(4^3) = -(4 \times 4 \times 4) = -64$

$(-4)^3 = (-4) \times (-4) \times (-4) = -64$

$-(-4)^3 = -[(-4) \times (-4) \times (-4)] = 64$

Pay close attention to where the negative signs are placed.

Ex. $(-2)^3(-5) - (12) \div 3 =$ → The exponent 3 is odd, so the first product is negative.

$(-2)^3(-5) - (-12) \div 3 = (-8)(-5) - (-12) \div 3 = 40 - (-4) = 44$

© Kumon Publishing Co., Ltd.

Practice It

1 **Calculate the answer for each of the following problems.**   14 points each

(1) $\dfrac{\frac{2}{3}}{\frac{8}{9}} =$

(2) $\dfrac{-\frac{2}{3}}{1\frac{1}{4}} =$

Remember to place parentheses around the numerator or denominator if necessary.

Convert decimals to fractions if it makes the question easier to calculate.

(3) $\dfrac{-2 + \frac{3}{4}}{3\frac{1}{2}} =$

(4) $\dfrac{-0.2 + \left(-\frac{1}{3}\right)}{\frac{3}{4} - \left(-1\frac{5}{6}\right)} =$

Count the number of negative signs first. Then determine the answer.

(5) $-1\frac{2}{3} - \left[\left(-\frac{5}{6}\right) \times 3\right] \div 1\frac{1}{4}$

$=$

(6) $(-0.4)^2 \div \left[\left(-3\frac{2}{5}\right) - (-5)\right] - 2\frac{1}{2}$

$=$

2 **The temperature on Monday is −2.5 degrees Celsius. Over the next 4 days, the temperature decreases $1\frac{1}{4}$ degrees each day. Then it increases by 3 degrees each day for 2 days. What is the final temperature?**   16 points

⟨Ans.⟩ _____

Values of Algebraic Expressions

Name

Date   /   /   Score   / 100

Remember It

Give these problems a try.

Evaluate each of the following expressions when $x = 4$ and $y = -\dfrac{2}{3}$.

1. $5x - \dfrac{8}{x} =$

2. $\dfrac{y}{x} + 5xy =$

Need a little help? Check out Review It before moving on.

⟨Ans.⟩ 1. 18   2. $-13\dfrac{1}{2}$

Review It

A **variable** is a symbol that is used in math to represent an unknown quantity. Letters, such as, x and y are often used as variables. To evaluate an expression with variables, substitute the given value for the variable in the expression.

Ex. $5x - \dfrac{8}{x} =$ → To find the value of the expression, we substitute 4 into x and simplify.

$$\text{Therefore } 5x - \dfrac{8}{x} = 5 \times 4 - \dfrac{8}{4}$$
$$= 20 - 2$$
$$= 18$$

Ex. $\dfrac{y}{x} + 5xy =$ → To find the value of the expression, we substitute 4 into x and substitute $-\dfrac{2}{3}$ into y

and simplify.

$$\text{Therefore } \dfrac{y}{x} + 5xy = \dfrac{-\dfrac{2}{3}}{4} + 5 \times 4 \times \left(-\dfrac{2}{3}\right)$$
$$= \left(-\dfrac{2}{3}\right) \times \dfrac{1}{4} + 5 \times 4 \times \left(-\dfrac{2}{3}\right)$$
$$= -\dfrac{1}{6} - \dfrac{40}{3}$$
$$= -\dfrac{1}{6} - 13\dfrac{1}{3}$$
$$= -13\dfrac{1}{2}$$

© Kumon Publishing Co., Ltd.

Practice It

1 Determine the value of each of the following expressions when $a = -3$.

14 points each

(1) $-a^4 =$

(2) $3a^2 - a - 2 =$

2 Determine the value of each of the following expressions when

$f = \dfrac{1}{2}$ **and** $g = -1$.

14 points each

(1) $\dfrac{f^2 - 2}{g + 3} =$

(2) $16f^2 - (g - f)^2 =$

3 Determine the value of each of the following expressions when $x = -2$, $y = 3$,

and $z = \dfrac{1}{4}$.

14 points each

(1) $xy - yz + x^2 - xz =$

(2) $(x - z)(y + x) =$

4 Determine the value of $\dfrac{xy^2}{z} - \dfrac{z - w}{x - y}$ **when** $x = -\dfrac{1}{2}$, $y = 2$, $z = 2\dfrac{1}{2}$, **and**

$w = -\dfrac{1}{4}$.

16 points

Algebra Quiz 2

Name
_____

Date _____ / _____ / _____   Score _____ / 100

1 **Calculate the answer for each of the following problems.**   7 points each

(1) $\dfrac{1}{2} \div \dfrac{1}{3} \times \dfrac{1}{4} - \dfrac{1}{2} + \dfrac{1}{3} =$

(2) $5 + 27 \div (1 + 2^3) =$

(3) $\dfrac{2}{3} + \dfrac{7}{2} \div \left(\dfrac{2}{5} \times 3\dfrac{3}{4}\right) =$

(4) $2 \div 8 + \left(\dfrac{1}{2}\right)^4 - \dfrac{1}{8} =$

(5) $\left(\dfrac{5}{21} \times 7 + 1\dfrac{1}{3}\right) \div 45 =$

(6) $8.4 \div \left(3\dfrac{2}{5} - \dfrac{11}{15}\right) + 3^2 =$

(7) $16 - 8 + 3\left[2^3 \div \left(-\dfrac{1}{4}\right)^2\right] \times \left(-\dfrac{1}{2}\right)^5 =$

(8) $(-5) \div 2 \times \left[6 - 9 \div 12 \times 3 - \dfrac{1}{2} \div \left(-\dfrac{1}{4}\right)^3\right]^0 =$

    © Kumon Publishing Co., Ltd.

2 Determine the value of each of the following expressions when $a = -\frac{1}{2}$, $b = 3$, and $c = 1\frac{1}{2}$.

7 points each

(1) $a^2 - (b^2 - c^2) =$

    (a) -14

    (b) $-6\frac{1}{2}$

    (c) $-7\frac{1}{2}$

    (d) $6\frac{1}{2}$

    (e) $7\frac{1}{2}$

(2) $(a \times b \div c)^2 =$

    (a) $-1\frac{1}{2}$

    (b) -1

    (c) 1

    (d) $1\frac{1}{2}$

    (e) $5\frac{1}{8}$

(3) $(a \times b \div c^2) =$

    (a) $-1\frac{1}{2}$

    (b) -1

    (c) $-\frac{2}{3}$

    (d) 1

    (e) $1\frac{1}{2}$

(4) $(a^2 - b) + (a - c)^2 =$

    (a) $1\frac{1}{4}$

    (b) $\frac{1}{2}$

    (c) $-1\frac{1}{4}$

    (d) $-\frac{1}{2}$

    (e) $-3\frac{3}{4}$

3 Kate has a party, and she estimates that each guest will eat $\frac{3}{4}$ of a small pizza. Let x equal the number of guests that she invites to the party, and answer each word problem.

8 points each

(1) Express the number of pizzas that are eaten by x guests.

⟨Ans.⟩ _____

(2) How many pizzas will be eaten if 6 guests come and an additional 3 pizzas are eaten by Kate's family?

⟨Ans.⟩ _____

© Kumon Publishing Co., Ltd.

10 Simplifying Algebraic Expressions 1

Algebra 12

Name _____

Date ____ / ____ / ____   Score _____ / 100

Remember It

Give these problems a try.

Simplify each of the following expressions.

1. $9x - 3y + 7 + 2y - 15x =$

2. $8a^2 + 9ab - \dfrac{1}{2}b^2 + 3 - 5 - \dfrac{2}{3}ab + \dfrac{2}{3}b^2 - 5a^2 =$

Need a little help? Check out Review It before moving on.

〈Ans.〉 1. $-6x - y + 7$ 2. $3a^2 + \dfrac{25}{3}ab + \dfrac{1}{6}b^2 - 2$

Review It

To simplify an algebraic expression, first combine **like terms**. Then arrange the terms in alphabetical order. For example, combine all x terms and combine all y terms, but do not combine x terms with y terms.

Ex. $9x - 3y + 7 + 2y - 15x =$ → **Like Terms**

$$9x + (-15x) = -6x$$
$$-3y + 2y = -y$$

Write the answer as $-y$, not $-1y$.

$$9x - 3y + 7 + 2y - 15x = -6x - y + 7$$

Multiplying variables creates a new term. So, a, ab, and a^2 are all different terms.

Ex. $8a^2 + 9ab - \dfrac{1}{2}b^2 + 3 - 5 - \dfrac{2}{3}ab + \dfrac{2}{3}b^2 - 5a^2 =$ → **Like Terms**

> Remember to use improper fractions and not mixed numbers.

$$8a^2 + (-5a^2) = 3a^2$$
$$9ab + \left(-\dfrac{2}{3}ab\right) = \dfrac{25}{3}ab$$
$$-\dfrac{1}{2}b^2 + \dfrac{2}{3}b^2 = -\dfrac{1}{6}b^2$$
$$3 + (-5) = -2$$

$$8a^2 + 9ab - \dfrac{1}{2}b^2 + 3 - 5 - \dfrac{2}{3}ab + \dfrac{2}{3}b^2 - 5a^2 = 3a^2 + \dfrac{25}{3}ab + \dfrac{1}{6}b^2 - 2$$

 © Kumon Publishing Co., Ltd.

Practice It

1 **Simplify each expression.**

12 points for (1)–(6), 14 points for (7) and (8)

(1) $7b - (-8b)$

$=$

(2) $3ab - \dfrac{1}{2}ab + 9a^2$

$=$

(3) $-\dfrac{1}{4}x + 2y - \dfrac{5}{6}x - \left(-\dfrac{1}{2}y\right)$

$=$

(4) $-2x^2 + \dfrac{3}{2}xy - (-x^2) + \left(-\dfrac{1}{4}xy\right)$

$=$

(5) $-9 + 7k^2 - \dfrac{2}{3}m + \dfrac{1}{2}k^2 + \dfrac{3}{4}m$

$=$

(6) $-\dfrac{1}{2}ab - \left(-\dfrac{3}{4}bc\right) + 8cd - 2bc + \dfrac{1}{3}cd - 4ab$

$=$

(7) $-6abc + \left(-\dfrac{1}{3}bd\right) + 5abc - (-2bd)$

$=$

(8) $9s^2 - 16t^2 - \dfrac{7}{3}st + 17t^2 - 10s^2 + \dfrac{3}{4}st$

$=$

Simplifying Algebraic Expressions 2

Name

Date   /   /

Score   / 100

 **Remember It**

Give these problems a try.

Simplify each expression.

1. $(2x + 3y) + (4x + 5y) =$

2. $(9m^2 + 2t^2) - (5m^2 + 10t^2) =$

3. $\left(\dfrac{1}{3}a - \dfrac{1}{2}b\right) - \left(-\dfrac{1}{4}a + \dfrac{2}{3}b\right) =$

Need a little help? Check out Review It before moving on.

⟨**Ans.**⟩ **1.** $6x + 8y$ **2.** $4m^2 - 8t^2$ **3.** $\dfrac{7}{12}a - \dfrac{7}{6}b$

 Review It

First rewrite the expression into a form with no parentheses. Then combine like terms to get the final answer.

Ex. $(2x + 3y) + (4x + 5y) = 2x + 3y + 4x + 5y$

$\qquad\qquad\qquad\qquad = 6x + 8y$

A subtraction sign before parentheses is equivalent to multiplying by -1 and should therefore be distributed across the parentheses.

Ex. $(9m^2 + 2t^2) - (5m^2 + 10t^2) = 9m^2 + 2t^2 - 5m^2 - 10t^2$

$\qquad\qquad\qquad\qquad\qquad\quad = 4m^2 - 8t^2$

Ex. $\left(\dfrac{1}{3}a - \dfrac{1}{2}b\right) - \left(-\dfrac{1}{4}a + \dfrac{2}{3}b\right) = \dfrac{1}{3}a - \dfrac{1}{2}b + \dfrac{1}{4}a - \dfrac{2}{3}b$

$\qquad\qquad\qquad\qquad\qquad\qquad = \dfrac{4}{12}a + \dfrac{3}{12}a - \dfrac{3}{6}b - \dfrac{4}{6}b$

$\qquad\qquad\qquad\qquad\qquad\qquad = \dfrac{7}{12}a - \dfrac{7}{6}b$

 © *Kumon Publishing Co., Ltd.*

Practice It

1 Simplify each expression.

15 points for (1)–(4), 20 points for (5) and (6)

(1) $(x - 7y) + (4x + 12y)$

=

(2) $(8a - b - 4c) + (2a - 6b + 3c)$

=

Write the correct sign when removing the parentheses.

(3) $(4k + 2m) - (5k + m)$

=

(4) $\left(\dfrac{5}{2}p^2 - 7q\right) - \left(-3p^2 - \dfrac{9}{4}q\right)$

=

(5) $(-8x - 2y + 3z) - (9x - 7y + 2z)$

=

(6) $\left(3a^2 + \dfrac{5}{2}ab - b^2\right) - \left(-\dfrac{7}{4}a^2 + 4ab + \dfrac{3}{5}b^2\right)$

=

Simplifying Algebraic Expressions 3

Name _____

Date ____ / ____ / ____   Score ____ / 100

Remember It

Give these problems a try.

Simplify each expression by using the Distributive Property.

1. $3(4x + 5y) =$

2. $5a + 2(4a - 7b) =$

3. $-\left(\dfrac{1}{2}k^2 + 3k\right) - 2\left(k^2 - 7k\right) =$

Need a little help? Check out Review It before moving on.

⟨**Ans.**⟩ **1.** $12x + 15y$ **2.** $13a - 14b$ **3.** $-\dfrac{5}{2}k^2 + 11k$

Review It

Distributive Property	The **Distributive Property** allows you to simplify the expression by multiplying the terms and removing the parentheses.	$a \times b$ $a(b + c) = ab + ac$ $a \times c$

Ex. $3(4x + 5y) =$ → Distribute the 3 by multiplying 3 by $4x$ and 3 by $5y$.
so, $3(4x + 5y) = 12x + 15y$.

The Distributive Property only applies to the number being multiplied by the sums or differences in parentheses.

Ex. $5a + 2(4a - 7b) =$ → Distribute the 2 by multiplying 2 by $4a$ and 2 by $-7b$.
Then combine like terms.
so, $5a + 2(4a - 7b) = 5a + 8a - 14b = 13a - 14b$.

Recall that a negative symbol in front of a term in parentheses is equivalent to multiplying by -1.

Ex. $-\left(\dfrac{1}{2}k^2 + 3k\right) - 2\left(k^2 - 7k\right) =$ → Distribute the -1 by multiplying -1 by $\dfrac{1}{2}k^2$ and -1 by $3k$.

Distribute the -2 by multiplying -2 by k^2 and -2 by $-7k$.
Then combine like terms.

so, $-\left(\dfrac{1}{2}k^2 + 3k\right) - 2\left(k^2 - 7k\right) = -\dfrac{1}{2}k^2 - 3k - 2k^2 + 14k$

$$= -\dfrac{5}{2}k^2 + 11k.$$

  © *Kumon Publishing Co., Ltd.*

Practice It

1 Simplify each expression.

12 points for (1)–(6), 14 points for (7) and (8)

(1) $x(y+z)$

=

(2) $2(3x-4y)$

=

Remember to combine like terms.

A number multiplied by its reciprocal has a product of 1.

(3) $12x+3(-x+5y)$

=

(4) $7x-2\left(\dfrac{1}{2}x-10\right)$

=

(5) $3(4a-b)+2(a+3b)$

=

(6) $4(2a+3b)-3(5a-b)$

=

(7) $-2\left(\dfrac{1}{3}x^2-\dfrac{1}{2}y^2\right)-4\left(\dfrac{2}{3}x^2+\dfrac{7}{2}y^2\right)$

=

(8) $-2\left(\dfrac{3}{2}a+4b-c\right)+\dfrac{1}{3}(-6a+2b-9c)$

=

Name

Date   Score

/   /   / 100

Remember It

Give these problems a try.

Solve each equation.

1. $x - 5 = 12$

2. $\frac{1}{2}x = 12$

3. $7x + 6 = 4x + 18$

Need a little help? Check out Review It before moving on.

⟨Ans.⟩ 1. $x = 17$ 2. $x = 24$ 3. $x = 4$

Review It

To solve an equation for a given variable, use **inverse operations** to isolate the variable. Inverse operations are operations that "undo" each other, or are opposites.

Ex. Solve for x: $x - 5 = 12$ → $x - 5 + 5 = 12 + 5$
$$x = 17$$

Check that the answer is correct by substituting $x = 17$ into the original equation:
Since $17 - 5 = 12$, we know that the answer is correct.

Ex. Solve for x: $\frac{1}{2}x = 12$ → Multiply both sides by the reciprocal of $\frac{1}{2}$, which is 2.
$$x = 24$$

Check that the answer is correct by substituting $x = 24$ into the original equation.

To isolate a variable in an equation with multiple terms, use inverse operations to sort like terms to either side of the equation. Then combine like terms and solve.

Ex. Solve for x: $7x + 6 = 4x + 18$ → $7x - 4x = 18 - 6$
$$3x = 12$$
$$x = 4$$

Check that the answer is correct by substituting $x = 4$ into the original equation.

© Kumon Publishing Co., Ltd.

Practice It

1 **Solve each equation.**

12 points for (1)–(6), 14 points for (7) and (8)

(1) $x + 3 = 9$

(2) $-6 + x = 7$

(3) $4x = -24$

(4) $-\dfrac{2}{3}x = 12$

Take note of negative numbers.

(5) $4x - 9 = -15$

(6) $5 - \dfrac{2}{3}x = 13$

Remember to sort the terms with x to one side and the terms without x to the other side.

Find the LCD for the variable terms and the LCD for the non-variable terms.

(7) $-3x - 5 = 3x + 9$

(8) $-\dfrac{1}{5}x + \dfrac{1}{4} = -\dfrac{1}{3}x - \dfrac{1}{2}$

Name _____

Date ____ / ____ / ____

Score _____ / 100

Remember It

Give these problems a try.

Solve each equation.

1. $2(3x - 7) = 4(-x + 9)$

2. $\frac{1}{2}x + \frac{1}{3} = \frac{1}{4}x - \frac{1}{6}$

3. $\frac{4x + 11}{3} = \frac{x - 1}{2}$

Need a little help? Check out Review It before moving on.

⟨Ans.⟩ 1. $x = 5$ 2. $x = -2$ 3. $x = -5$

Review It

When solving equations, you may need to simplify the expressions on one side of an equation before isolating the variable.

Ex. $2(3x - 7) = 4(-x + 9) \rightarrow 6x - 14 = -4x + 36$ Use the distributive property.

$\qquad\qquad\qquad\qquad\qquad 10x = 50$ Combine like terms.

$\qquad\qquad\qquad\qquad\qquad\quad x = 5$ Solve.

You may sometimes want to convert fractions to whole numbers to simplify. You can eliminate the denominators by multiplying each side by the LCD.

Ex. $\frac{1}{2}x + \frac{1}{3} = \frac{1}{4}x - \frac{1}{6} \rightarrow$ The LCD is 12.

$$12 \times \left(\frac{1}{2}x + \frac{1}{3}\right) = \left(\frac{1}{4}x - \frac{1}{6}\right) \times 12$$

$$6x + 4 = 3x - 2$$

$$x = -2$$

To remove the denominator and solve for x, we multiply each side by the LCM of the denominators. Since the LCM of 3 and 2 is 6, we multiply all the terms on both sides.

Ex. $\frac{4x + 11}{3} = \frac{x - 1}{2} \rightarrow$ The LCD is 6.

$$6 \times \left(\frac{4x + 11}{3}\right) = \left(\frac{x - 1}{2}\right) \times 6$$

$$2(4x + 11) = 3(x - 1)$$

$$x = -5$$

© Kumon Publishing Co., Ltd.

pp. 1–65
Algebra

pp. 67–151
Geometry

pp. 153–183
Probability & Statistics

pp. 185–197
Review

Practice It

1 Solve each equation.

12 points for (1)–(6), 14 points for (7) and (8)

Distribute the negative.

(1) $4(2x - 5) = -12$

(2) $-(3x - 4) = 2\left(\frac{1}{2}x + 6\right)$

(3) $-\frac{2}{3}x + \frac{1}{2} = \frac{2}{5} - \frac{3}{4}x$

(4) $\frac{3}{4}x - 6 = 2x + \frac{3}{2}$

(5) $\frac{3}{2} - 3x = \frac{5}{3} + \frac{1}{4}x$

(6) $-\frac{3}{8}x - \frac{5}{12} = -\frac{1}{6}x + \frac{1}{4}$

You can use the LCD to convert the fractions.

(7) $\frac{2x - 3}{4} = \frac{6x - 3}{3}$

(8) $\frac{-3x + 4}{5} = \frac{-x + 2}{3} - 2$

Solving Equations 3

Remember It

Give these problems a try.

1. Write each sentence as an equation and then solve.
(1) x times 3 is equal to -12.   (2) Subtracting $4x$ from 13 equals 1.

2. Write the following word problem as an equation and then solve.

Jack has 15 jellybeans and Jill has 3 jellybeans. Jack gives Jill x jellybeans. Jill now has twice the amount of jellybeans as Jack. How many jellybeans did Jack give Jill?

Need a little help? Check out Review It before moving on.

⟨**Ans.**⟩ **1.** (1) $x = -4$ (2) $x = 3$ **2.** $(3+x) = 2(15-x)$; Jack gave Jill 9 jellybeans.

Review It

Ex. Write the sentence "x times 3 is equal to -12" as an equation, then solve.

The phrase "x times 3" can be expressed using multiplication as: $3x$, so the sentence "x times 3 is equal to -12" can be rewritten as: $3x = -12$.
Thus, the answer is: $x = -4$.

Ex. Write the sentence "Subtracting $4x$ from 13 equals 1" as an equation, then solve.

The phrase "subtracting $4x$ from 13" can be expressed using subtraction as: $13 - 4x$,
so, "subtracting $4x$ from 13 equals 1" can be rewritten as: $13 - 4x = 1$.
Thus, the answer is: $x = 3$.

Ex. Jack has 15 jellybeans and Jill has 3 jellybeans. Jack gives Jill x jellybeans. Jill now has twice the amount of jellybeans as Jack. How many jellybeans did Jack give Jill?

If Jack gives Jill x jellybeans, now Jack has a new total of $(15 - x)$ jellybeans and Jill has a new total of $(3 + x)$. Since Jill now has twice the amount of jellybeans as Jack, the equation describing this situation is: $(3 + x) = 2(15 - x)$. So, the answer is: $x = 9$ jellybeans.

  © Kumon Publishing Co., Ltd.

 **Practice It**

1 **Write each sentence as an equation and then solve.**　20 points each

(1)　The sum of $2x$ and 5 is equal to 19.

(2)　x divided by 4 is $\dfrac{3}{2}$.

2 **Write each of the following word problems as an equation and then solve.**
20 points each

(1)　Susie buys several bags of clay. The total weight of all the bags is 96 pounds. If Susie buys a total of 8 bags, how much does each bag weigh?

⟨**Ans.**⟩ _____

(2)　Lee receives a small box of markers and erasers that weighs 46 ounces. Each marker weighs 3 ounces and each eraser weighs 2 ounces. If there are 8 markers, how many erasers are there?

⟨**Ans.**⟩ _____

(3)　Jinni buys several apples and oranges and purchases a total of 39 fruits. There are 5 fewer oranges than apples. How many apples did she buy?

⟨**Ans.**⟩ _____

Quiz
Algebra Quiz 3
Algebra 18

Name

Date _____ / _____ / _____

Score _____ / 100

1 **Simplify each expression.**   10 points each

(1) $(-2a + 3b) - \left(-\dfrac{1}{2}a - 4b\right) =$

    (a) $-\dfrac{5}{2}a + b$

    (b) $-\dfrac{5}{2}a + 7b$

    (c) $-\dfrac{3}{2}a + b$

    (d) $-\dfrac{3}{2}a + 7b$

(2) $\left(-\dfrac{1}{2}s + \dfrac{1}{2}t\right) - \left(\dfrac{3}{4}s - \dfrac{5}{6}t\right) =$

    (a) $-\dfrac{5}{4}s + \dfrac{4}{3}t$

    (b) $-\dfrac{3}{2}s + \dfrac{3}{2}t$

    (c) $\dfrac{5}{4}s - \dfrac{4}{3}t$

    (d) $\dfrac{3}{2}s - \dfrac{4}{3}t$

2 **Solve each equation.**   11 points each

(1) $x + \dfrac{5}{2} = -\dfrac{1}{4}x$

(2) $3x - 5 = 7x + 27$

(3) $-\left(2x - \dfrac{8}{3}\right) = 2\left(4 - \dfrac{3}{2}x\right)$

(4) $\dfrac{-2x + 3}{2} - 1 = \dfrac{7 - 2x}{5}$

3   Write each of the following word problems as an equation, and then solve.

9 points each

(1) Bobbi receives a crate of t-shirts that weighs 68 ounces. If each t-shirt weighs 4 ounces, how many t-shirts are in the crate?

⟨**Ans.**⟩ _____

(2) There are a total of 32 students in Troy's class. If there are 8 more girls than boys, how many girls are there in the class?

⟨**Ans.**⟩ _____

(3) In 15 years, Mike will be 4 times his current age. What is Mike's current age?

⟨**Ans.**⟩ _____

(4) Sue is currently 7 years old. Arthur is currently 20 years old. In how many years will Arthur be twice as old as Sue?

⟨**Ans.**⟩ _____

© Kumon Publishing Co., Ltd.   37

Remember It

Give these problems a try.

Solve the following system of equations for both x and y.

$$\begin{cases} 7x + 2y = 12 & \cdots ① \\ 3x + 2y = 4 & \cdots ② \end{cases}$$

Need a little help? Check out Review It before moving on.

⟨**Ans.**⟩ $(x, y) = (2, -1)$

Review It

Two linear equations with the same variables are called **simultaneous linear equations**.

You can solve for the variables by subtracting one equation from the other. This method is known as the **Elimination Method**, which can also be called the **Subtraction Method** or the **Addition Method**.

Ex.

$$\begin{cases} 7x + 2y = 12 & \cdots ① \\ 3x + 2y = 4 & \cdots ② \end{cases}$$

Step 1: Number each equation.

$$① - ②: \quad \begin{array}{r} 7x + 2y = 12 \quad \cdots ① \\ -)\ 3x + 2y = 4 \quad \cdots ② \\ \hline 4x \qquad = 8 \\ x = 2 \end{array}$$

Step 2: Remove a variable by subtracting one equation from the other.

Substitute this into ②:

$$6 + 2y = 4$$
$$2y = -2$$
$$y = -1$$

Step 3: Substitute the value of the variable into either original equation (usually the simpler one) to solve for the other variable.

$$(x, y) = (2, -1)$$

Step 4: Write your answer.

© Kumon Publishing Co., Ltd.

pp. 1–65
Algebra

pp. 67–151
Geometry

pp. 153–183
Probability & Statistics

pp. 185–197
Review

 Practice It

1 **Solve each of the following systems of equations.**

15 points for (1)–(4), 20 points for (5) and (6)

(1)

$$\begin{cases} 5x + 3y = 14 \\ x - 3y = -8 \end{cases}$$

(2)

$$\begin{cases} 2x - y = -7 \\ 2x - 3y = -13 \end{cases}$$

What operation should you use first?

(3)

$$\begin{cases} 5x - 2y = -3 \\ x + 2y = 9 \end{cases}$$

(4)

$$\begin{cases} -2x + 5y = -21 \\ -2x - y = 9 \end{cases}$$

(5)

$$\begin{cases} 6x - 5y = -17 \\ 6x + y = 7 \end{cases}$$

(6)

$$\begin{cases} -x + \dfrac{3}{2}y = -1 \\ \dfrac{1}{4}x - \dfrac{3}{2}y = \dfrac{5}{2} \end{cases}$$

Name

Date   /   /

Score   /100

Remember It

Give these problems a try.

Solve the following system of equations.

$$\begin{cases} 4x + 3y = 10 & \cdots① \\ 5x + 2y = 9 & \cdots② \end{cases}$$

Need a little help? Check out Review It before moving on.

⟨**Ans.**⟩ $(x, y) = (1, 2)$

Review It

Ex.

$$\begin{cases} 4x + 3y = 10 & \cdots① \\ 5x + 2y = 9 & \cdots② \end{cases}$$

Step 1: Number each equation.

$①×2:$ $8x + 6y = 20$ $\cdots③$
$②×3:$ $15x + 6y = 27$ $\cdots④$

Step 2: Multiply one equation by a constant and number the new equation. In this example, we multiplied equation ① by 2 and called it equation ③. Likewise, we multiplied equation ② by 3 and called it equation ④.

$③ - ④:$

$$\begin{aligned} 8x + 6y &= 20 \quad \cdots③ \\ -)\ 15x + 6y &= 27 \quad \cdots④ \\ \hline -7x \qquad &= -7 \\ x &= 1 \end{aligned}$$

Step 3: Remove a variable by using the Elimination Method.

Substitute this into ②:

$$5 + 2y = 9$$
$$2y = 4$$
$$y = 2$$

Step 4: Substitute the value of the variable into either original equation (usually the simpler one) to solve for the other variable.

$(x, y) = (1, 2)$

Step 5: Write your answer.

pp. 1–65
Algebra

pp. 67–151
Geometry

pp. 153–183
Probability & Statistics

pp. 185–197
Review

Practice It

1 **Solve each of the following systems of equations.**

15 points for (1)–(4), 20 points for (5) and (6)

(1)
$$\begin{cases} 2x + 3y = -3 \\ 5x + 4y = -11 \end{cases}$$

(2)
$$\begin{cases} -4x - 3y = 17 \\ 5x - 7y = 11 \end{cases}$$

(3)
$$\begin{cases} x - \dfrac{3}{2}y = -8 \\ 3x + \dfrac{5}{2}y = 11 \end{cases}$$

(4)
$$\begin{cases} 4x + 9y = 2 \\ 10x + 3y = -\dfrac{3}{2} \end{cases}$$

In order to solve equations, it may be easier to first rearrange and/or simplify the equations into the form $ax + by = c$.

(5)
$$\begin{cases} 2y = -3x + 11 \\ -5y = 8x - 12 \end{cases}$$

(6)
$$\begin{cases} 2(3x + y) = 9x + 2y - 6 \\ -4x - 3y = 5(-7x - 2y + 4) \end{cases}$$

Remember It

Solve the following equation.

$$\begin{cases} y = 3x - 5 & \cdots ① \\ 5x - 2y = 7 & \cdots ② \end{cases}$$

Need a little help? Check out Review It before moving on.

⟨Ans.⟩ $(x, y) = (3, 4)$

Review It

You can also use a method called the **Substitution Method**. In this method, you substitute one equation into the other equation to eliminate one variable and solve for the remaining variable.

Ex.

$$\begin{cases} y = 3x - 5 & \cdots ① \\ 5x - 2y = 7 & \cdots ② \end{cases}$$

Step 1: Number each equation.

Substitute ① into ②:

$$5x - 2(3x - 5) = 7$$
$$5x - 6x + 10 = 7$$
$$-x = -3$$
$$x = 3$$

Step 2: Substitute one equation into the other to remove a variable.

Substitute this into ①:

$$y = 9 - 5$$
$$y = 4$$

Step 3: Substitute the value of the variable into either original equation (usually the simpler one) to solve for the other variable.

$$(x, y) = (3, 4)$$

Step 4: Write your answer.

© Kumon Publishing Co., Ltd.

pp. 1–65
Algebra

pp. 67–151
Geometry

pp. 153–183
Probability & Statistics

pp. 185–197
Review

Practice It

1 **Solve each of the following equations.**

15 points each

(1)

$$\begin{cases} x = 2y + 9 \\ 3x + 5y = 5 \end{cases}$$

(2)

$$\begin{cases} 4x - y = -4 \\ 8x - 3y = -14 \end{cases}$$

2 **Use the following methods to solve the following system of equations:**

$$\begin{cases} 2x - 3y = 11 \\ -3x - y = -11 \end{cases}$$

15 points each

(1) Elimination Method

(2) Substitution Method

3 **Use the following methods to solve the following system of equations:**

$$\begin{cases} 2x + 4y = -5 \\ 5x - 3y = 7 \end{cases}$$

20 points each

(1) Elimination Method

(2) Substitution Method

Name _____

Date _____ / _____ / _____   Score _____ / 100

Remember It

Solve each of the following inequalities.

1. $x - 6 < 2$

2. $5x + 4 \geq 2x - 8$

3. $-2x > 14$

4. $x - 5 \leq 4x - 17$

Need a little help? Check out Review It before moving on.

⟨**Ans.**⟩ 1. $x < 8$ 2. $x \geq -4$ 3. $x < -7$ 4. $x \geq 4$

Review It

Solving inequalities is much like solving equations. You must isolate the variables using inverse operations.

Ex. $x - 6 < 2 \;\rightarrow\; x < 2 + 6$ Isolate the variable.
$\phantom{x - 6 < 2 \;\rightarrow\;} x < 8$ Add to solve.

Just like in solving equations, sort the terms to either side of the inequality based on whether or not it has a variable.

Ex. $5x + 4 \geq 2x - 8 \;\rightarrow\; 5x - 2x \geq -8 - 4$ Sort to isolate the variable.
$ x \geq -4$ Combine like terms.

However, remember that when we are multiplying or dividing an inequality by a negative number, we reverse the inequality sign.

Ex. $-2x > 14 \;\rightarrow\; \dfrac{-2x}{-2} < \dfrac{14}{-2}$ Divide to isolate the variable.

Reverse the inequality sign.

$ x < -7$ Reduce to solve.

Ex. $x - 5 \leq 4x - 17 \;\rightarrow\; -3x \leq -12$ Sort and combine like terms.
$ x \geq 4$ Divide to isolate the variable. Then reverse the inequality sign.

© Kumon Publishing Co., Ltd.

Practice It

1 **Solve each of the following inequalities.**   12 points each

(1) $4x + 5 > 29$

(2) $-2x + 5 \leq 11$

(3) $4x + 8 \geq x - 9$

(4) $-5x + \dfrac{1}{2} \leq -7x + 3$

First, multiply both sides by the LCM of 2 and 3.

(5) $\dfrac{x - 1}{2} < \dfrac{x - 4}{3}$

(6) $\dfrac{2x + 5}{2} \geq \dfrac{6x - 8}{4}$

2 **Write each word problem as an inequality, and then solve.**   14 points each

(1) x plus 8 is less than 5 times x.

〈Ans.〉 _____

(2) Three times the difference of $2x$ and 5 is greater than half the sum of $-3x$ and 5.

〈Ans.〉 _____

Remember It

Give these problems a try.

1. There are 15 red-colored candies and 40 blue-colored candies in a bag. Use this information to answer each of the following questions.
    (1) Write the ratio of red-colored candies to blue-colored candies, using the smallest integers possible. Then express the ratio as a fraction.
    (2) Use a fraction to express the ratio of red-colored candies to the total number of candies in the bag.

2. The ratio of the number of boys in a classroom to the number of girls in the classroom is $\frac{2}{3}$. If there are 18 girls in the classroom, how many boys are there?

Need a little help? Check out Review It before moving on.

⟨Ans.⟩ 1.(1) 3:8, $\frac{3}{8}$ (2) $\frac{3}{11}$ 2. 12 boys

Review It

The proportion of A to B is represented as 3 : 2.
This is also called the **ratio** of A to B, and it is shown by the expression $A : B = 3 : 2$.

```
        3                       2
  ┌─────────────┐        ┌──────────┐
A │   │   │   │          B │   │   │
  └─────────────┘          └──────────┘
```

The **value of a ratio** is the first term divided by the second term.

```
  ┌───┐          ┌─────────────┐
C │   │        D │   │   │   │   │   │        C : D = 2 : 5   →   2 ÷ 5 = 2/5
  └───┘          └─────────────┘
```

$$C : D = 2 : 5 \rightarrow 2 \div 5 = \frac{2}{5}$$

Ratios can represent a part to another part or a part to the whole (or total amount). A ratio is expressed with the smallest integer.

Ex. There are 15 red-colored candies and 40 blue-colored candies in a bag.

red : blue → 15 : 40 → reduce to 3 : 8 or $\frac{3}{8}$

red : total → 15 : 55 → reduce to 3 : 11 or $\frac{3}{11}$

You can solve problems with ratios by representing the unknown value with a variable.

Ex. The ratio of the number of boys in a classroom to the number of girls in the classroom is $\frac{2}{3}$. If there are 18 girls in the classroom, how many boys are there? → Let x = the number of boys in the classroom.

boys : girls → $x : 18$ or $\frac{x}{18}$ → $\frac{x}{18} = \frac{2}{3}$ → The number of boys in the classroom is: 12.

Ex. The ratio of cats to dogs in a park is less than $\frac{3}{4}$. If there are 8 dogs in the park, how many cats could there be in the park? → Let x = the number of cats in the park.

cats : dogs → $x : 8$ or $\frac{x}{8}$ → $\frac{x}{8} < \frac{3}{4}$ → There are less than 6 cats in the park.

Practice It

1 There are 72 students enrolled in a university class. 56 students show up to class one day. Use this information to answer each of the following questions.

20 points each

(1) Write the ratio of the number of students who showed up to class to the total number of students in the class, using the smallest integers possible. Then express the ratio as a fraction.

⟨Ans.⟩ _____

(2) Write the ratio of the number of students who showed up to class to the number of students who did not show up to class, using the smallest integers possible. Then express the ratio as a fraction.

⟨Ans.⟩ _____

2 The ratio of chefs to customers in a restaurant is less than or equal to $\frac{1}{12}$. If there are 60 customers in the restaurant, how many possible chefs are there?

20 points

⟨Ans.⟩ _____

3 The ratio of birds in a zoo to the total number of animals in the zoo is greater than $\frac{3}{8}$. If there is a total number of 200 animals in the zoo, how many possible birds are there?

20 points

⟨Ans.⟩ _____

4 The ratio of Sam's age to Kai's age is $\frac{3}{2}$. If Kai is 12 years old, how old is Sam?

20 points

⟨Ans.⟩ _____

1 **Use the following methods to solve the following system of equations:**

$$\begin{cases} -8x + 5y = 1 \\ 4x + 3y = -6 \end{cases}$$

12 points each

(1) Elimination Method

(2) Substitution Method

2 **Use the following methods to solve the following system of equations:**

$$\begin{cases} 7x + 4y = 1 \\ 5x = -3y \end{cases}$$

12 points each

(1) Elimination Method

(2) Substitution Method

3 **Solve each of the following inequalities.**

12 points each

(1) $3x - 5 \geq 7x + 8$

(a) $x \leq -\dfrac{3}{4}$ (b) $x \leq -\dfrac{13}{4}$ (c) $x \geq -\dfrac{13}{4}$ (d) $x \geq \dfrac{3}{4}$

(2) $\dfrac{2x - 3}{6} \leq \dfrac{3x + 8}{4}$

(a) $x \geq -6$ (b) $x \leq -6$ (c) $x \geq -3.6$ (d) $x \leq -3.6$

pp. 1–65
Algebra

pp. 67–151
Geometry

pp. 153–183
Probability & Statistics

pp. 185–197
Review

4 The ratio of the number of adults on a subway to the number of children on the subway is less than $\frac{3}{4}$. If there are 28 children on the subway, how many possible adults are there?

14 points

⟨Ans.⟩ _____

5 The ratio of Elliot's age to Jayden's age is greater than $\frac{3}{5}$. If Jayden is 45 years old, what is Elliot's possible age?

14 points

⟨Ans.⟩ _____

Name _____

Date _____ / _____ / _____   Score _____ / 100

Remember It

Give these problems a try.

Write the coordinates of each of the points on the coordinate plane below.

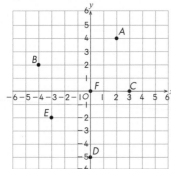

1. Point A: _____

2. Point B: _____

3. Point C: _____

4. Point D: _____

5. Point E: _____

6. Point F: _____

Need a little help? Check out Review It before moving on.

⟨Ans.⟩ **1.** (2, 4) **2.** (−4, 2) **3.** (3, 0) **4.** (0, −5) **5.** (−3, −2) **6.** (0, 0)

Review It

On a **coordinate plane**, the **x-axis** is the horizontal number line, and the **y-axis** is the vertical number line. Each point is expressed as an **ordered pair** of numbers called the **x-coordinate** and the **y-coordinate**. The coordinates are always expressed in the order (x, y). The x-axis and y-axis meet at a point called the **origin**. The coordinates of the origin are $(0, 0)$.

Ex. Write the coordinates of each of the points on the coordinate plane from Remember It, above.
Point A: The x-coordinate is 2. The y-coordinate is 4. → (2, 4)
Point B: The x-coordinate is −4. The y-coordinate is 2. → (−4, 2)
Point C: The x-coordinate is 3. The y-coordinate is 0. → (3, 0)
Point D: The x-coordinate is 0. The y-coordinate is − 5. → (0, −5)
Point E: The x-coordinate is −3. The y-coordinate is −2. → (−3, −2)
Point F: The x-coordinate is 0. The y-coordinate is 0. → (0, 0)
        Point F is located at the *origin*.

Ex. Find each value of y for the equation $y = -2x + 1$ by completing the table below. Then use the completed table to graph the equation.

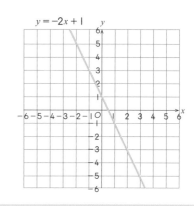

x	-2	$-\dfrac{3}{2}$	-1	$-\dfrac{1}{2}$	0	$\dfrac{1}{2}$	1	$\dfrac{3}{2}$	2
y	5	4	3	2	1	0	−1	−2	−3

To find the y-coordinate when $x = -2$, substitute -2 for x into the equation $y = -2x + 1$. → $y = 4 + 1 = 5$. Repeat for all the points.

Practice It

1 **Write the coordinates of each of the following points.**   5 points each

(1) Point A: _____

(2) Point B: _____

(3) Point C: _____

(4) Point D: _____

(5) Point E: _____

(6) Point F: _____

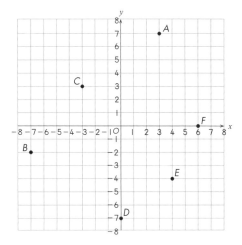

2 **Plot each of the points on the coordinate plane.**   5 points each

(1) Point A: $(-3, 2)$

(2) Point B: $(-4, -1)$

(3) Point C: $(4, 0)$

(4) Point D: $(0, -5)$

(5) Point E: $\left(\dfrac{5}{2}, -\dfrac{7}{2}\right)$

(6) Point F: $(0, 0)$

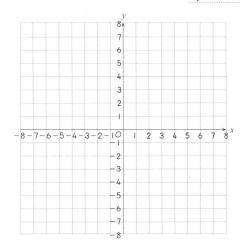

3 **Complete the table below to find each value of y for the equation $y = -\dfrac{1}{2}x - 3$. Then use the completed table to graph the equation.**   5 points each

x	−3	−2	−1	0	1	2	3
y							

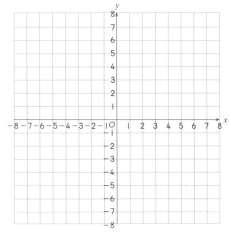

Graphs 2

Name

Date   /   /

Score   /100

Remember It

Give these problems a try.

Use the graph to answer each of the following questions.

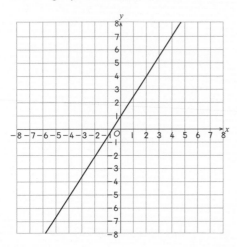

1. What is the y-intercept?

2. What is the slope?

3. What is the equation of the line?

Need a little help? Check out Review It before moving on.

⟨Ans.⟩ 1. 1   2. $\frac{3}{2}$ 3. $y = \frac{3}{2}x + 1$

Review It

- The y-**intercept** of a line is the value on the y-axis where the line crosses the y-axis.
- The **slope** of a line describes the steepness of a line. The formula for slope is: **slope** $= \dfrac{\textbf{rise}}{\textbf{run}}$.
- The formula of a line is $y = mx + b$, where m represents the slope and b represents the y-intercept.

   Ex. Use the graph to find the y-intercept, slope, and the equation of the line.

   y-intercept → The line intersects the y-axis at $(0, 1)$.

   $\quad\quad\quad$ y-intercept $= 1$

   Slope → The line rises 3 units vertically for every 2 units it runs

   $\quad\quad\quad$ horizontally. The slope $= \dfrac{3}{2}$

   Equation → $y = \dfrac{3}{2}x + 1$

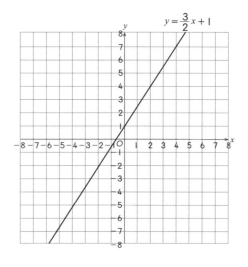

- Lines with a positive slope increase from left to right.

- Lines with a negative slope decrease from left to right.

  © *Kumon Publishing Co., Ltd.*

pp. 1–65
Algebra

pp. 67–151
Geometry

pp. 153–183
Probability & Statistics

pp. 185–197
Review

Practice It

1 **For each of the given graphs, indentify the _y_-intercept, slope, and equation.**

10 points each

(1) _y_-intercept: _____

     Slope: _____

     Equation: _____

(2) _y_-intercept: _____

     Slope: _____

     Equation: _____

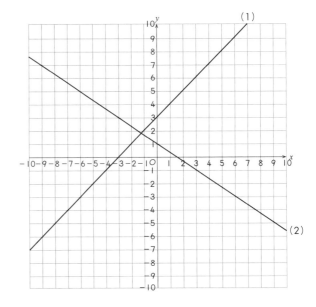

2 **Draw the graph of each of the following equations on the coordinate plane below.**

10 points each

(1) $y = \dfrac{4}{3}x + 4$

(2) $y = -\dfrac{5}{2}x - 1$

(3) $y = -x - 3$

(4) $y = \dfrac{3}{2}x - 1$

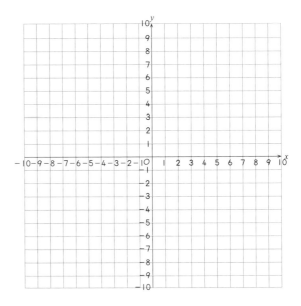

© _Kumon Publishing Co., Ltd._

Name _____

Date _____/_____/_____   Score _____/ 100

Remember It

Give these problems a try.

1. Which relation is a function?

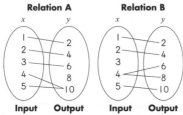

Relation A   Relation B

2. What are the domain and range of the function below?
$\{(1, 3), (2, 4), (3, 5), (4, 6)\}$

3. Which of the graphs below represent a function? Circle all the graphs that represent a function.

A   B   C   D

Need a little help? Check out Review It before moving on.

⟨**Ans.**⟩ **1.** Relation A   **2.** Domain: {1, 2, 3, 4}; Range: {3, 4, 5, 6}   **3.** A, B, and D

Review It

A **relation** is the relationship between two sets of data or a set of ordered pairs. A **function** is a special type of relation where one variable in the ordered pair depends on the other. In a function, each *input* can only have exactly one *output*.

Ex. Which relation is a function? (Refer to Remember It **1.**)

In Relation A, even though the inputs 4 and 5 have the same output, 10, each input has exactly one output. So, Relation A is a function. In Relation B, the input 4 has two outputs, so it is not a function.

In a function, all of the input values are in a set called the **domain**. Each value in the domain is matched with exactly one output value. The set containing the output values is called the **range**.

Ex. What are the domain and range of the function : $\{(1, 3), (2, 4), (3, 5), (4, 6)\}$

The domain of the set of all x-coordinates in the function → {1, 2, 3, 4}
The range of the set of all y-coordinates in the function → {3, 4, 5, 6}

In a **Vertical Line Test**, a vertical line drawn anywhere on the graph of a relation passes through two points shows that it is not a function.

Ex. Is the relation a function?

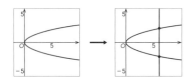

The relation is not a function because a vertical line that passes through two points can be drawn on the graph of the relation.

Practice It

1 **Determine if the following relations are functions. Label each relation with an F for a function and an N for not a function.** 14 points each

（1）

Input	Output
2	2
3	3
4	4

〈Ans.〉_____

（2）

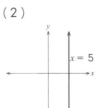

〈Ans.〉_____

（3）

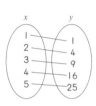

〈Ans.〉_____

（4）

〈Ans.〉_____

（5） Imagine the graph of the relation mapped in （4）. What will the graph look like?

〈Ans.〉_____

2 **Give the domain and range for each of the functions below.** 10 points each

（1） $\{(1, 6), (2, 7), (3, 8), (4, 9), (5, 10)\}$

Domain: _____

Range: _____

（2） $\{(10, 3), (9, 2), (8, 1), (7, 0), (6, -1)\}$

Domain: _____

Range: _____

（3）

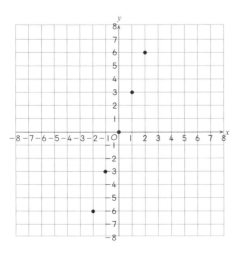

Domain: _____

Range: _____

Remember It

Give these problems a try.

Use the graph below to find each of the following.

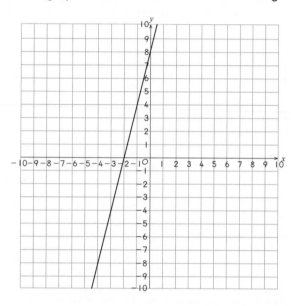

1. Slope: _____

2. y-intercept: _____

3. Equation: _____

Need a little help? Check out Review It before moving on.

⟨Ans.⟩ 1. 4   2. 8   3. $y = 4x + 8$

Review It

Recall that the slope of a line can be found by finding the change in y divided by the change in x.

Ex. Find the slope of the line graphed in Remember It.

The points $(-2, 0)$ and $(0, 8)$ are on the line.

$$\frac{y_2 - y_1}{x_2 - x_1} = \frac{8 - 0}{0 - (-2)} = \frac{8}{2}$$

This simplifies to $\frac{4}{1}$ or 4.

So, the slope is 4.

If the relation between x and y can be expressed in the form $y = mx + b$, then the equation is called a **linear function**.

Ex. Is the relation graphed in Remember It a function?

The y-intercept is 8 and the slope is 4, so the equation is: $y = 4x + 8$

Since the relation can be expressed in the form $y = mx + b$, the relation is a function.

pp. 1–65
Algebra

pp. 67–151
Geometry

pp. 153–183
Probability & Statistics

pp. 185–197
Review

Practice It

1 **Use the graph on the right to answer each of the following questions.**   8 points each

(1) When the value of y is 0, what is the value of x?

⟨**Ans.**⟩ $x =$ _____

(2) When the value of x is 0, what is the value of y?

⟨**Ans.**⟩ $y =$ _____

(3) As the value of x increases, do the values of y increase or decrease?

⟨**Ans.**⟩ _____

(4) As the values of x increase by 3, how much do the values of y decrease by?

⟨**Ans.**⟩ _____

(5) Another way to express this is to say:
As the values of x increase by 1, how much do the values of y decrease by?

⟨**Ans.**⟩ _____

(6) So, what is the slope?

⟨**Ans.**⟩ _____

Be careful of the sign!

(7) What is the equation of the line?

⟨**Ans.**⟩ _____

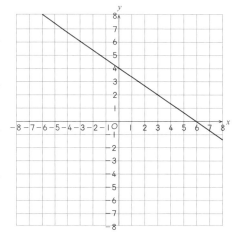

2 **Use the graph on the right to find each of the following.**   11 points each

(1) y-intercept: _____

(2) Slope: _____

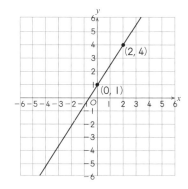

3 **A line passes through the points (−4, 1) and (4, −5).**   11 points each

(1) Find the equation of the line.

⟨**Ans.**⟩ _____

(2) Graph the equation on the coordinate plane on the right.

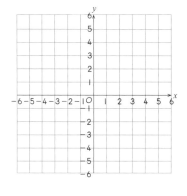

© Kumon Publishing Co., Ltd.   57

Remember It

Give these problems a try.

Given the system of equations: $\begin{cases} 2x - y = 5 & \cdots ① \\ 3x + 2y = 4 & \cdots ② \end{cases}$

1. Rewrite the equations in slope-intercept form: $y = mx + b$.
2. Find the intersection point by using each of the following methods.
   (1) By graphing   (2) Using algebra

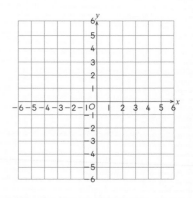

Need a little help? Check out Review It before moving on.

⟨**Ans.**⟩ **1.** ① $y = 2x - 5$ ② $y = -\frac{3}{2}x + 2$ **2.** See examples in Review It; Intersection point: $(2, -1)$

Review It

The **standard form of a line** is given as $ax + by = c$. You can determine the slope and y-intercept of a line given in standard form by using inverse operations to isolate the y variable and rewrite the equation in **slope-intercept form**: $y = mx + b$.

Ex. Given the system of equations: $\begin{cases} 2x - y = 5 & \cdots ① \\ 3x + 2y = 4 & \cdots ② \end{cases}$

Rewrite the equations in slope-intercept form: $y = mx + b$.

$2x - y = 5 \quad \rightarrow \quad y = 2x - 5$

$3x + 2y = 4 \quad \rightarrow \quad 2y = -3x + 4$

$\qquad\qquad\qquad\qquad y = -\frac{3}{2}x + 2$

Ex. Find the intersection point by graphing.

Based on the slope-intercept form of ①, the y-intercept is $b = -5$, and the slope is $m = 2$.

Likewise, for the slope-intercept form of ②, the y-intercept is $b = 2$, and the slope is $m = -\frac{3}{2}$.

Graph the lines, you can see the intersection point is $(2, -1)$.

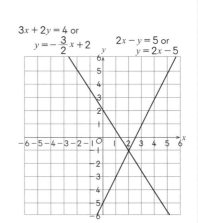

Ex. Find the intersection point using algebra.

Substitute ① into ② → ② becomes $3x + 2(2x - 5) = 4$.

$3x + 4x - 10 = 4$

$\qquad\qquad 7x = 14$

$\qquad\qquad x = 2$ and $y = -1$.

So, the intersection point is $(2, -1)$.

© Kumon Publishing Co., Ltd.

pp. 1–65
Algebra

pp. 67–151
Geometry

pp. 153–183
Probability & Statistics

pp. 185–197
Review

Practice It

1 Find the slope of each of the following lines.   10 points each

(1) Slope: $m =$ _____

(2) Slope: $m =$ _____

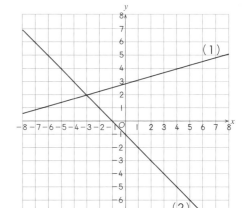

2 Find the equation of the line and graph it on the coordinate plane.   10 points each

(1) A line passes through $(-4, 3)$ and has a slope of $-\dfrac{1}{3}$.

Equation: _____

(2) A line passes through the points $(4, 7)$ and $(-2, -3)$.

Equation: _____

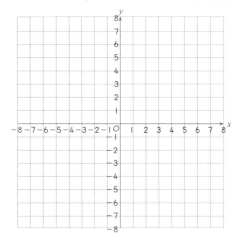

3 Given the following system, find the intersection point.   20 points each

$$\begin{cases} 2x + 2y = 3 & \cdots ① \\ 3x - 4y = -20 & \cdots ② \end{cases}$$

(1) By graphing   (2) Using algebra

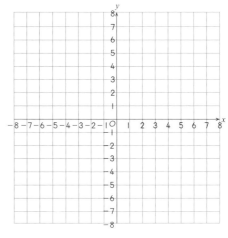

Name _____

Date ____ / ____ / ____   Score _____ / 100

Remember It

Give these problems a try.

1. Draw and label the graph $y = 2$ on the coordinate plane.
2. What is the slope of $y = 2$?
3. Draw and label the graph of $x = -3$ on the coordinate plane.
4. What is the slope of $x = -3$?

Need a little help? Check out Review It before moving on.

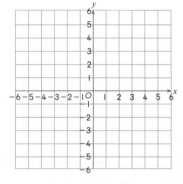

⟨**Ans.**⟩ **1.** See example in Review It.   **2.** The slope is 0.   **3.** See example in Review It.   **4.** The slope is undefined.

Review It

The equation for a **horizontal line** is $y = a$ (where a represents a number). Horizontal lines have a slope of 0.

Ex. Draw and label the graph $y = 2$ on the coordinate plane and find the slope.

For every x-value, $y = 2$.
Plot two points with a y-value of 2.
→ For example $(0, 2)$ and $(3, 2)$.
Then connect to form a horizontal line.

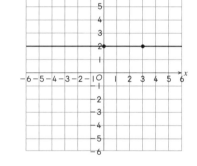

Since the y-coordinates of all the points of a horizontal line are the same, the rise is 0. So, the slope of all horizontal lines is 0 and the slope of $y = 2$ is 0.

The equation for a **vertical line** is $x = a$ (where a represents a number).
The slope of a vertical line does not exist.

Ex. Draw and label the graph of $x = -3$ on the coordinate plane and find the slope.

For every y-value, $x = -3$.
Plot two points with an x-value of -3.
→ For example $(-3, 0)$ and $(-3, 3)$.
Then connect to form a vertical line.

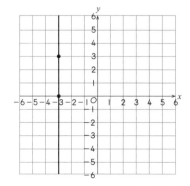

Recall that the slope of all vertical lines is undefined because the x-coordinates of all the points are the same. The run is 0, so the slope is undefined.
So, the slope of $x = -3$ is undefined.

© Kumon Publishing Co., Ltd.

Practice It

1 **Graph each of the following equations on the coordinate plane.**   10 points each

(1) $y = 5$

(2) $-2x - 7 = 0$

> First, rewrite the equation into $y = mx + b$ form.

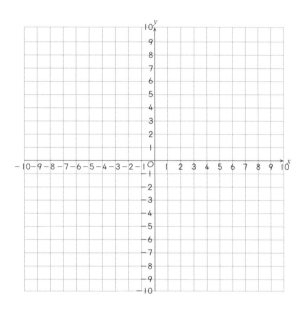

2 **Graph each of the following equations on the coordinate plane.**   20 points each

(1) $x = -6$

(2) $2y = -10$

(3) $-4y + 14 = 0$

(4) $8x - 20 = 0$

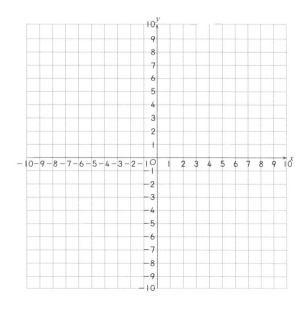

Name

Date _____ / _____ / _____   Score _____ / 100

Remember It

Give these problems a try.

1. Find the line parallel to $y = \frac{1}{2}x + 3$ that passes through $(4, -1)$.

2. Find the line perpendicular to $y = \frac{2}{3}x - 7$ that passes through $(-6, 5)$.

Need a little help? Check out Review It before moving on.

⟨**Ans.**⟩ **1.** $y = \frac{1}{2}x - 3$ **2.** $y = -\frac{3}{2}x - 4$

Review It

Parallel lines are lines that have the same slope but different y-intercepts. Parallel lines do not have any points of intersection.

Ex. Find the line parallel to $y = \frac{1}{2}x + 3$ that passes through $(4, -1)$.

$m = \frac{1}{2}$, so the slope of a parallel line must also be $\frac{1}{2} \rightarrow y = \frac{1}{2}x + b$.

Substitute the point $(4, -1)$ into the equation to solve for b.
The line is: $y = \frac{1}{2}x - 3$

Perpendicular lines have **negative reciprocal** slopes.

Ex. Find the line perpendicular to $y = \frac{2}{3}x - 7$ that passes through $(-6, 5)$.

$m = \frac{2}{3}$, so the slope of a perpendicular line must be $-\frac{3}{2} \rightarrow y = -\frac{3}{2}x + b$.

Substitute $(-6, 5)$ into the equation to solve for b.
The line is: $y = -\frac{3}{2}x - 4$

© Kumon Publishing Co., Ltd.

pp. 1–65
Algebra

pp. 67–151
Geometry

pp. 153–183
Probability & Statistics

pp. 185–197
Review

Practice It

1 **Solve the following problems.**

25 points each

(1) Find the line parallel to $3x - 4y = -2$ that passes through $(4, 6)$.

⟨Ans.⟩ _____

(2) Graph both equations from (1) on the coordinate plane.

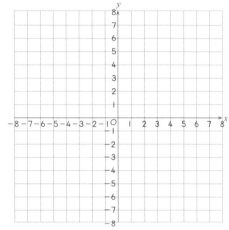

2 **Solve the following problems.**

25 points each

(1) Find the line perpendicular to $2x + y = 3$ that passes through $(-5, 4)$.

⟨Ans.⟩ _____

(2) Graph both equations from (1) on the coordinate plane.

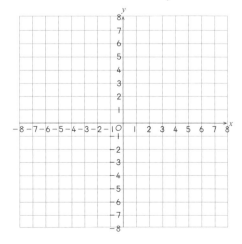

1 Draw each of the following equations on the coordinate plane to the right.

6 points each

(1) $y = 2x + 4$

(2) $y = \dfrac{4}{3}x - 2$

(3) $y = -3x + 1$

(4) $y = -5$

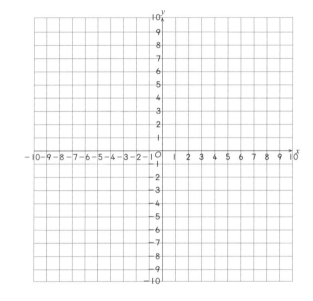

2 Draw each of the following equations on the coordinate plane to the right.

6 points each

(1) $2x + 6y = 3$

(2) $6x = 2y + 9$

(3) $4x = -8$

(4) $3y - 12 = 0$

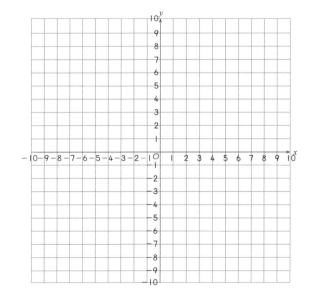

© Kumon Publishing Co., Ltd.

3 **Give the domain and range for each of the functions below.** 12 points each

(1) $\{(1, 2), (2, 4), (3, 6), (4, 8), (5, 10)\}$

Domain: _____

Range: _____

(2) $\{(12, 3), (11, 2), (10, 1), (9, 0), (8, -1)\}$

Domain: _____

Range: _____

4 **Which is the equation of the line that is parallel to** $3x + 2y = 6$ **and passes through (0, 4)?** 14 points

(a) $y = -\frac{1}{2}x + 6$

(b) $y = -\frac{3}{2}x + 4$

(c) $y = -\frac{3}{2}x + 6$

(d) $y = -\frac{3}{2}x + 8$

5 **Which is the equation of the line that is perpendicular to** $-5x + 2y = 9$ **and passes through (10, −7)?** 14 points

(a) $y = \frac{2}{5}x + 3$

(b) $y = \frac{1}{5}x + 9$

(c) $y = -\frac{2}{5}x - 3$

(d) $y = \frac{1}{5}x - 9$

Memo

Kumon Math Workbooks

Grades **7** & **8**

Are You Ready for High School Math?

Geometry

Table of Contents

Name

Date

Score

/ / /100

Remember It

Give these problems a try.

Express the following statements with the correct symbol.

   1.   Line *AB*

   2.   Line segment *AB*

   3.   Ray *AB*

Need a little help? Check out Review It before moving on.

⟨Ans.⟩ 1. $\overleftrightarrow{AB}$ 2. $\overline{AB}$ 3. $\overrightarrow{AB}$

Review It

Although numerous lines can pass through one point, there is only one line that can pass through two points. A **line** has no endpoints and extends infinitely in both directions. It can be expressed using any two points on the line.

A **ray** is a portion of a line that has one endpoint but extends infinitely in a single direction. A ray can be expressed with an arrow in the direction that extends infinitely.

A **line segment** represents the bounded area of a line. It has two endpoints with a determined length.

Two lines are **parallel** when they do not **intersect**.

Two lines are **perpendicular** when they intersect and create a right angle.

Line $AB \rightarrow \overleftrightarrow{AB}$

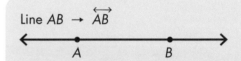

Line segment $AB \rightarrow \overline{AB}$

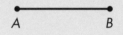

Ray $AB \rightarrow \overrightarrow{AB}$

Ray $BA \rightarrow \overrightarrow{BA}$

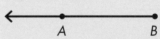

Parallel lines ℓ and $m \rightarrow \ell \parallel m$

Perpendicular lines p and $q \rightarrow p \perp q$

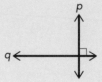

pp. 1–65
Algebra

pp. 67–151
Geometry

pp. 153–183
Probability & Statistics

pp. 185–197
Review

Practice It

1 **Use points A to E on the right to answer the questions below.**   10 points each

(1) Draw $\overleftrightarrow{AB}$.

(2) Draw $\overline{CD}$.

(3) Draw $\overrightarrow{CE}$.

(4) Draw $\overrightarrow{DB}$.

• A   • D

• C

• B

• E

2 **Draw each of the following figures. Line f is provided for you.**   30 points each

(1) $g \parallel f$ (Draw line g).

(2) $f \perp h$ (Draw line h).

The positional relationship of two lines on the
same plane is either parallel or intersecting.

f

Geometric Notation 2
Angles and Triangles

Name _____

Date ____/____/____   Score _____/100

Remember It

Give these problems a try.

Express the following statements by using the correct symbol(s).

1. Angle *A*
2. Write two other ways to represent angle *ABC*.
3. Angle *ABC* measures 90 degrees.
4. Angle *BAC* and angle *BCA* are congruent.
5. $\overline{AB}$ and $\overline{BC}$ are congruent.

Need a little help? Check out Review It before moving on.

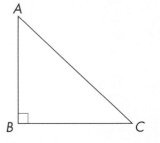

⟨Ans.⟩ 1. ∠A   2. ∠B or ∠CBA   3. m∠ABC = 90°   4. ∠BAC ≅ ∠BCA   5. $\overline{AB} ≅ \overline{BC}$ (or AB ≅ BC)

Review It

Angles are represented by the ∠ symbol.	**Ex.** Angle *A* → ∠*A* (Triangles are represented by the △, such as △*ABC*.)
Angles can be represented by a single letter or by all the letters and points that create the angle.	**Ex.** Write two other ways to represent angle *ABC*. → ∠*B* or ∠*ABC* or ∠*CBA* However, expressing it in other ways, such as ∠*BCA* or ∠*ACB*, would be incorrect.
When describing the measure of an angle, place an *m* before it.	**Ex.** Angle *ABC* measures 90 degrees. → *m*∠*ABC* = 90°
When two angles are **congruent**, we express the statement by using the ≅ symbol.	**Ex.** Angle *BAC* and angle *BCA* are congruent. → ∠*BAC* ≅ ∠*BCA*
When two sides are congruent, we express the statement by using the ≅ symbol.	**Ex.** $\overline{AB}$ and $\overline{BC}$ are congruent. → $\overline{AB} ≅ \overline{BC}$ (or AB ≅ BC) You can represent the measurement of a line segment using only use the endpoints without the line above.

© Kumon Publishing Co., Ltd.

pp. 1–65
Algebra

pp. 67–151
Geometry

pp. 153–183
Probability & Statistics

pp. 185–197
Review

Practice It

1 Express the following statements with the correct symbol based on the shape below.

(1)–(6)15 points each, (7)10 points

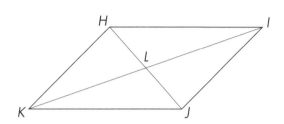

(1)   Angles *HLK* and *ILJ* are congruent.

⟨**Ans.**⟩ _____

(2) $\overline{IJ}$ and $\overline{HK}$ are congruent.

⟨**Ans.**⟩ _____

(3) $\overline{KL}$ and $\overline{LI}$ are congruent.

⟨**Ans.**⟩ _____

(4)   Angles *IJK* and *KHI* are congruent.

⟨**Ans.**⟩ _____

(5)   The sum of angles *LKH*, *LHI*, *LIJ*, and *LJK* equals to 180°.

⟨**Ans.**⟩ _____

(6) $\overline{HI}$ and $\overline{KJ}$ are congruent.

⟨**Ans.**⟩ _____

(7)   How many triangles are there in the figure?

Some triangles are different sizes!

⟨**Ans.**⟩ _____

Name _____

Date ___ / ___ / ___   Score ___ / 100

Remember It

Give these problems a try.

Sort the shapes shown into the categories below.

1. Right Triangle: _____
2. Isosceles Triangle: _____ , _____
3. Equilateral Triangle: _____
4. Trapezoid: _____

5. Parallelogram: _____ , _____ , _____
6. Rhombus: _____ , _____
7. Rectangle: _____ , _____
8. Square: _____

Need a little help? Check out Review It before moving on.

⟨Ans.⟩ 1. E   2. A, G   3. G   4. B   5. C, D, F, H   6. D, F   7. D, H   8. D

Review It

An **isosceles triangle** is a triangle with two congruent sides.

An **equilateral triangle** is a triangle with three congruent sides.

A **right triangle** is a triangle with a right angle.

A **parallelogram** is a quadrilateral with two pairs of parallel, congruent sides.

A **rhombus** is a parallelogram with four congruent sides.

A **rectangle** is a parallelogram with four right angles.

A **square** is a parallelogram with four congruent sides and four right angles.

A **trapezoid** is a quadrilateral that has only one pair of parallel sides.

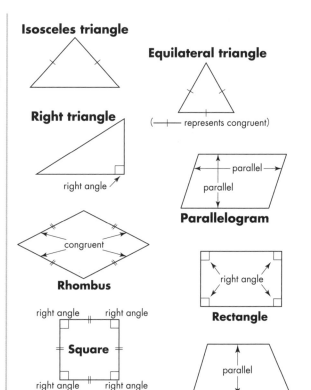

 **Practice It**

1 **Write all the shape categories that meet each of the descriptions below.**

20 points each

(1) A quadrilateral that has four right angles

〈**Ans.**〉 _____ , _____

(2) A quadrilateral that has only one pair of parallel sides

〈**Ans.**〉 _____

(3) A quadrilateral that has two pairs of parallel sides

〈**Ans.**〉 _____ , _____ , _____ , _____

Classifying Quadrilaterals

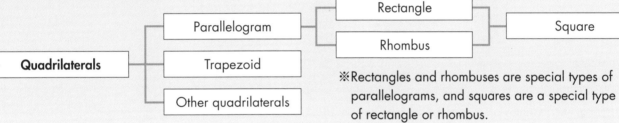

※Rectangles and rhombuses are special types of parallelograms, and squares are a special type of rectangle or rhombus.

2 **Write all the shape categories that each of the shapes below belong to.**

20 points each

(1)

〈**Ans.**〉 _____ , _____

(2)

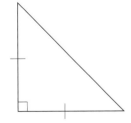

〈**Ans.**〉 _____ , _____

31 Geometry Basics 2
Angles

Geometry 4

Name

Date   /   /

Score   /100

Remember It

Give these problems a try.

Sort the angles shown into the categories below.

1. Acute Angles:
2. Obtuse Angles:
3. Right Angles:
4. Vertical Angles:

Need a little help? Check out Review It before moving on.

⟨Ans.⟩ **1.** ∠A, ∠C, ∠H   **2.** ∠B, ∠D, ∠E   **3.** ∠F, ∠G   **4.** ∠A and ∠C, ∠B and ∠D

Review It

A **right angle** is an angle that measures exactly 90°.

An **acute angle** is an angle that measures less than 90°.

An **obtuse angle** is an angle that measures greater than 90°.

Complementary angles add up to 90°, and combine to form a right angle.

Supplementary angles add up to 180°, forming a straight line, also known as a **straight angle**.

Acute angle < 90°

Right angle = 90°

Obtuse angle > 90°
< 180°

Right angle = 90°

Straight angle = 180°

180°

When two straight lines intersect, the opposite angles at the intersection point are congruent and called **vertical angles**.

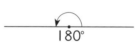

When a line intersects two other lines, the angles that are in the same relative position are called **corresponding angles**.

When a line intersects two other lines, the angles that are on opposite sides of the line are called **alternate angles**.

Corresponding angles

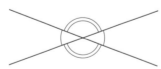

Alternate angles

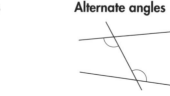

Practice It

1 Use the figure to find all the following angles.   20 points each

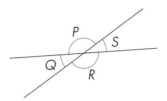

(1) What angle is congruent to ∠P?

⟨**Ans.**⟩ _____

(2) What angles are supplementary to ∠P?

⟨**Ans.**⟩ _____

(3) What is the sum of the measurement of ∠Q and ∠R?

⟨**Ans.**⟩ _____

2 Lines *m* and *n* are parallel.
Use the figure to find all the following angles.   20 points each

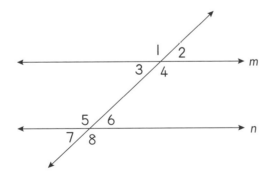

When there are two parallel lines cut by a **transversal**, the corresponding angles are congruent, and the alternate angles are also congruent!

(1) Which angles are congruent to ∠1?   ⟨**Ans.**⟩ _____

(2) Which angles are congruent to ∠2?   ⟨**Ans.**⟩ _____

32

Geometry Basics 3
Perimeter, Area, and Volume

Geometry 5

Name

Date   /   /

Score   / 100

Remember It

Give these problems a try.

Find the values using the figures below.

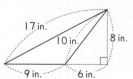

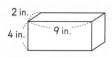

1. What is the perimeter of the triangle?
2. What is the area of the square?
3. What is the length of the diameter of the circle?
4. What is the volume of the rectangular prism?

Need a little help? Check out Review It before moving on.

⟨Ans.⟩ 1. 36 in.   2. 100 cm²   3. 10 cm   4. 72 in.³

Review It

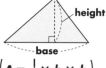

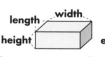

$(A = b \times h)$ $\left(A = \frac{1}{2} \times b \times h\right)$ $(d = 2 \times r)$ $(V = \ell \times w \times h)$ $(V = a^3)$
where a represents the edge

The **perimeter** of any shape is the total length of all its sides.

> **Ex.** What is the perimeter of the triangle above? → $P = 17 + 10 + 9 = 36$ in.

The **area** of a parallelogram is the base times the height.

The **area** of a triangle is the base times the height divided by two. The base and height must be perpendicular to each other.

> **Ex.** What is the area of the square above? → $A = b \times h = 10 \times 10 = 100$ cm²

> **Ex.** What is the area of the triangle above? → $A = \frac{1}{2} \times 8 \times 9 = 36$ in.²

The length of a **diameter** of a circle is the radius times two.

> **Ex.** What is the length of the diameter of the circle above? → $d = 2 \times r = 2 \times 5 = 10$ cm

> The diameter of the circle is 10 cm, so each side of the square measures 10 cm. The perimeter of the square is:
> $P = 10 + 10 + 10 + 10 = 40$ cm

The **volume** of a rectangular prism is length times width times height.

> **Ex.** What is the volume of the rectangular prism above? → $V = \ell \times w \times h = 9 \times 2 \times 4 = 72$ in.³

pp. 1–65
Algebra

pp. 67–151
Geometry

pp. 153–183
Probability & Statistics

pp. 185–197
Review

Practice It

1 **Find the area of the shaded region of the figure.**   25 points

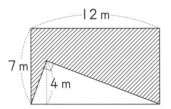

⟨Ans.⟩ _____

2 **Find the volume of the cube.**   25 points

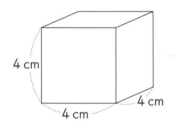

The volume of a cube is edge times edge times edge.

⟨Ans.⟩ _____

3 **Use the net to find the following answers.**   25 points each

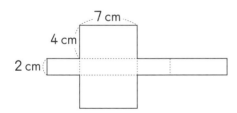

（1） What is the perimeter of the net?   ⟨Ans.⟩ _____

（2） What is the volume of the rectangular prism?   ⟨Ans.⟩ _____

33 Line Symmetry and Rotational Symmetry

Geometry 6

Name _____

Date ___/___/___   Score ___/100

Remember It

Give these problems a try.

Each center of symmetry is labeled in the figures shown.

A    B   C   D   E

Use the figures to answer each of the following questions.

1. Which of the shapes have line symmetry?
2. Which of the shapes have rotational symmetry?

Need a little help? Check out Review It before moving on.

⟨Ans.⟩ 1. A, C, D, E   2. A, C

Review It

A shape has **line symmetry** if it can be folded in half along a line so that both halves perfectly overlap. That means that the form of the shape is the same on both sides of one axis. The line along which you could fold a shape into two halves is called the **line of symmetry**.

Ex. Which of the shapes in Review It have line symmetry? → A, C, D, and E can each be folded in half and have perfectly overlapping parts.

A 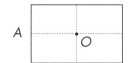   B    C   D   E

If a shape is rotated 180° around a center point, and the rotated figure perfectly overlaps with the original shape, then it has **rotational symmetry**. The point around which you can rotate a shape with rotational symmetry is called the **center of symmetry**.

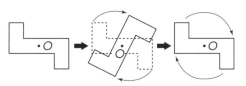

If you connect corresponding points in a figure with rotational symmetry, those lines will pass through the center of symmetry. The length from the center of symmetry to each corresponding point is equal.

Ex. Which of the shapes in Review It have rotational symmetry? → A and C can both be rotated 180° around a center point and perfectly overlap the original shape, so they both have rotational symmetry. The other shapes do not.

A    B    C   D   E

---

78   © Kumon Publishing Co., Ltd.

pp. 1–65
Algebra

pp. 67–151
Geometry

pp. 153–183
Probability & Statistics

pp. 185–197
Review

Practice It

1 Draw all the possible lines of symmetry of the figure.

30 points

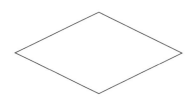

2 Which of the following shapes have rotational symmetry?

30 points

(a) (b) (c) (d)

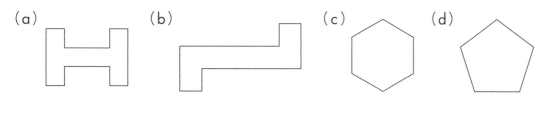

⟨**Ans.**⟩ _____

3 Plot the center of symmetry, *O*, on the figure.

40 points

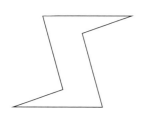

In a figure with rotational symmetry, lines connecting all the corresponding vertices cross through the center of symmetry.

34 Circles 1
Circumference and Area

Geometry 7

Remember It

Give these problems a try.

Answer each of the following questions, using the figure. Use π in your answer.

5 cm

1. What is the circumference of the circle?
2. What is the area of the circle?

Need a little help? Check out Review It before moving on.

⟨Ans.⟩ 1. 10π cm   2. 25π cm²

Review It

The perimeter of a circle is called the **circumference**. The ratio of the circumference of a circle to the diameter is called **pi**, or **π**.

The length of the circumference is equal to the diameter times π.

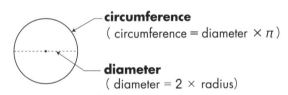

circumference
(circumference = diameter $\times \pi$)

diameter
(diameter = 2 × radius)

$C = 2 \times \pi \times \text{(radius)}$

Ex. What is the circumference of a circle with a 5 cm radius? →
$C = 2\pi r = 2 \times \pi \times 5 = 10\pi$ cm

The **area of a circle** is equal to the radius squared times π.

radius

$A = \pi \times \text{(radius)}^2$

Ex. What is the area of a circle with a 5 cm radius? →
$A = \pi r^2 = \pi \times (5)^2 = 25\pi$ cm²

   © Kumon Publishing Co., Ltd.

Practice It

1 Find the circumference and area of the circle.

15 points each

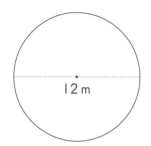

12 m

(1) Circumference: 〈Ans.〉 _____

(2) Area: 〈Ans.〉 _____

2 Find the perimeter and area of the shape.

15 points each

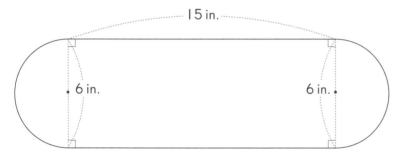

15 in.

6 in.   6 in.

(1) Perimeter: 〈Ans.〉 _____

(2) Area: 〈Ans.〉 _____

3 Find the perimeter and the area of the shape.

20 points each

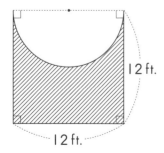

12 ft.

12 ft.

(1) Perimeter: 〈Ans.〉 _____

(2) Area: 〈Ans.〉 _____

Name _____

Date ____/____/____   Score ____/100

Remember It

Give these problems a try.

Answer each of the following questions about the sector below. Use π in your answers.

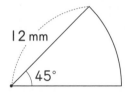

12 mm

45°

1. What is the length of the arc?

2. What is the perimeter of the sector?

3. What is the area of the sector?

Need a little help? Check out Review It before moving on.

⟨Ans.⟩ 1. 3π mm   2. (24 + 3π) mm   3. 18π mm²

Review It

A part of the circumference is called an **arc**. The angle between two radii of a sector is called a **central angle**.

The **length of the arc** is proportional to the measure of the central angle. For example, if the center angle is doubled, the arc length will be doubled.

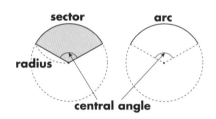

sector   arc

radius

central angle

The formula of the **length of an arc** is: $\ell = 2\pi \times (\text{radius}) \times \dfrac{\text{central angle}}{360}$	**Ex.** What is the length of the arc from Remember It above? $\ell = 2\pi \times 12 \times \dfrac{45}{360} = 3\pi$ mm
The region bound by an arc and two radii of a circle is called a **sector**. The formula of the **perimeter of a sector** is: $P = 2 \times (\text{radius}) + \text{arc length}$	**Ex.** What is the perimeter of the sector from Remember It above? $P = 2 \times 12 + 3\pi = (24 + 3\pi)$ mm
The formula of the **area of a sector** is: $A = \pi \times (\text{radius})^2 \times \dfrac{\text{central angle}}{360}$	**Ex.** What is the area of the sector from Remember It above? $A = \pi \times (12)^2 \times \dfrac{45}{360} = 18\pi$ mm²

Practice It

1 Answer each of the following questions about the sector. Use π in your answers.

(1)(2)15 points each, (3)20 points

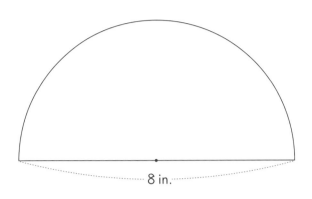

8 in.

> The area of a sector is proportional to the measure of the central angle.

(1) What is the length of the arc?

⟨**Ans.**⟩ _____

(2) What is the perimeter of the sector?

⟨**Ans.**⟩ _____

(3) What is the area of the sector?

⟨**Ans.**⟩ _____

2 Answer each of the following questions about the sector. Use π in your answers.

(1)(2)15 points each, (3)20 points

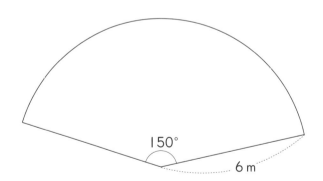

150°

6 m

(1) What is the length of the arc?

⟨**Ans.**⟩ _____

(2) What is the perimeter of the sector?

⟨**Ans.**⟩ _____

(3) What is the area of the sector?

⟨**Ans.**⟩ _____

© Kumon Publishing Co., Ltd.

Name

Date   Score

/   /   / 100

Remember It

Give these problems a try.

Given the triangle. Draw a perpendicular bisector of each of the sides of the triangle.

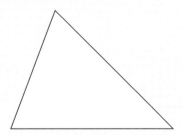

Need a little help? Check out Review It before moving on.

⟨**Ans.**⟩ See example in Review It.

Review It

If point M on $\overline{AB}$ and $\overline{AM} \cong \overline{BM}$, then point M is called the **midpoint**. Midpoint M of $\overline{AB}$ bisects $\overline{AB}$.

A **perpendicular bisector** is a straight line that passes through the midpoint of a line segment and is perpendicular to the line segment.

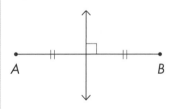

An **angle bisector** is a ray that divides an angle into two congruent angles.
$\angle AOE \cong \angle BOE \cong \frac{1}{2} \angle AOB$

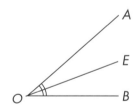

Ex. Draw a perpendicular bisector of each side of the triangle.

The perpendicular bisector of each side must pass through the midpoint of each side and also be perpendicular to each side.

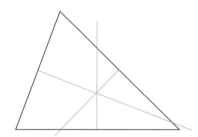

© Kumon Publishing Co., Ltd.

pp. 1–65
Algebra

pp. 67–151
Geometry

pp. 153–183
Probability & Statistics

pp. 185–197
Review

Practice It

1 **Given ∠AOB. Draw the angle bisector of ∠AOB.**

40 points

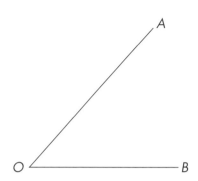

The angle bisector of ∠AOB divides ∠AOB into two congruent angles.

2 **Given △ABC, where △ABC is an isosceles triangle.**
Draw the following in order:

10 points each

(1) Draw a perpendicular line from vertex A to side BC in △ABC.

Notice that side AB is congruent to side AC.

(2) Label point M as the intersection point of the perpendicular

line and side BC.

(3) Draw a circle with radius BM around point M.

Notice that point C is on the circumference of the circle.

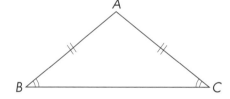

A midpoint divides a line segment into two congruent parts.

3 **Given △DEF, where △DEF is an isosceles triangle.**
Draw the following in order:

10 points each

(1) Draw the angle bisector of ∠EDF.

(2) Label point M as the intersection point of the angle bisector

and side EF.

(3) Draw a circle with radius EM around point M.

Notice that point F is on the circumference of the circle.

In an isosceles triangle, the perpendicular
bisector of the base also bisects the vertex angle.

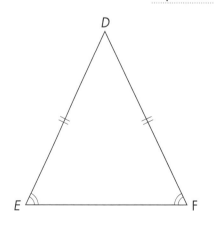

Name

Date / /

Score / 100

1 Find the perimeter and the area of the figure.
Use π in your answer.

10 points each

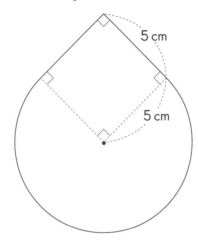

5 cm

5 cm

⟨**Ans.**⟩ Perimeter: , Area:

2 Find all the following angles, using the figure, where lines *a* and *b* are parallel.

5 points each

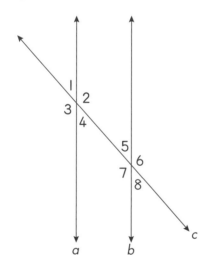

(1) Which angle(s) is/are vertical angle(s) with ∠2?

　(a) ∠1　(b) ∠3　(c) ∠4　(d) ∠5　(e) ∠6

(2) Which angle(s) is/are corresponding angle(s) with ∠2?

　(a) ∠1　(b) ∠3　(c) ∠4　(d) ∠5　(e) ∠6

(3) Which angle(s) is/are alternate angle(s) with ∠2?

　(a) ∠4　(b) ∠5　(c) ∠6　(d) ∠7　(e) ∠8

(4) Which angle(s) is/are congruent to ∠2?

　(a) ∠1　(b) ∠3　(c) ∠5　(d) ∠6　(e) ∠7

© Kumon Publishing Co., Ltd.

3 **Draw all the possible lines of symmetry of the figure.**   30 points

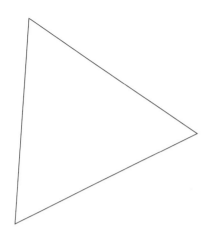

4 **Answer each of the following questions about the figure below. Use π in your answers.**   6 points each

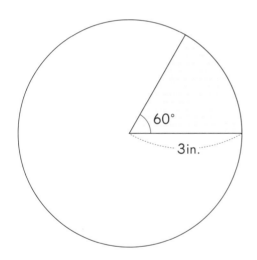

(1) What is the circumference of the circle?   ⟨**Ans.**⟩ _____

(2) What is the area of the circle?   ⟨**Ans.**⟩ _____

(3) What is the length of the arc of the shaded sector?   ⟨**Ans.**⟩ _____

(4) What is the perimeter of the shaded sector?   ⟨**Ans.**⟩ _____

(5) What is the area of the shaded sector?   ⟨**Ans.**⟩ _____

Lines, Planes, and Distance in Space

Name

Date   Score

/   /   / 100

Remember It

Give these problems a try.

Answer the questions about the rectangular prism, where the surfaces are each contained within a plane.

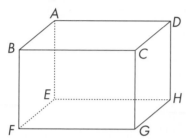

1. State all the edges parallel to $\overline{AB}$.
2. State all the surfaces perpendicular to plane *ABFE*.
3. State all the edges in a skewed position with $\overline{BF}$.

Need a little help? Check out Review It before moving on.

⟨Ans.⟩ 1. $\overline{DC}$, $\overline{EF}$, $\overline{HG}$ 2. ABCD, BCGF, EFGH, AEHD   3. $\overline{AD}$, $\overline{CD}$, $\overline{EH}$, $\overline{GH}$

Review It

The place where lines and planes intersect or are parallel is called the **space**. In the space:
• two planes can either be parallel or intersect
• a line and a plane can:

       1. have the line included in the plane
       2. be parallel to each other
       3. intersect each other

• a line and a different line can:

       1. be parallel when one plane contains two straight lines
       2. intersect when one plane contains two straight lines
       3. be in a skewed position when there is not one plane containing two straight lines

It follows that two lines are either **parallel** or **intersecting** if there is a plane that contains both lines. Two lines are in a **skewed position** if there is no plane that contains both lines.

Ex. State all the edges parallel to $\overline{AB}$. → $\overline{AB} \parallel \overline{DC} \parallel \overline{EF} \parallel \overline{HG}$ since they all lie on a plane with $\overline{AB}$, even though it is not the same plane for each.

Ex. State all edges in a skewed position with $\overline{BF}$. → $\overline{AD}$, $\overline{CD}$, $\overline{EH}$, and $\overline{GH}$ are in a skewed position to $\overline{BF}$.

Two planes are **perpendicular** if they create a right angle where they intersect.

Ex. State all the surfaces perpendicular to plane *ABFE*. → The surfaces *ABCD*, *BCGF*, *EFGH*, and *AEHD* are perpendicular to *ABFE*.

pp. 1–65
Algebra

pp. 67–151
Geometry

pp. 153–183
Probability & Statistics

pp. 185–197
Review

 Practice It

1 **Answer the questions about the rectangular prism.**

20 points each

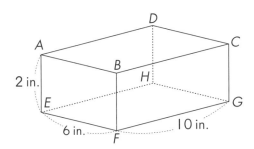

(1) Find the distance between $\overline{AB}$ and $\overline{DC}$.

⟨**Ans.**⟩ _____

(2) Find the distance between point G and $ABCD$.

⟨**Ans.**⟩ _____

(3) Find the distance between $\overline{BC}$ and $AEHD$.

⟨**Ans.**⟩ _____

In a rectangular prism, three sets of opposing faces are parallel and three straight lines intersect perpendicularly at each of the eight vertices.

2 **Line ℓ is perpendicular to both plane P and line m. Answer the questions about the figure below.**

20 points each

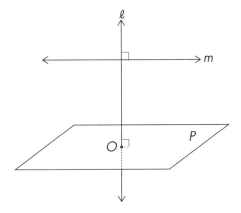

(1) State the relationship between line m and plane P. Use the relevant mathematical symbol.

⟨**Ans.**⟩ _____

(2) Line n is on plane P and crosses through point O. State the relationship between line ℓ and line n. Use the relevant mathematical symbol.

⟨**Ans.**⟩ _____

Name _____

Date ___/___/___   Score _____/100

Remember It

Give these problems a try.

Answer each of the following questions about the triangular prism.

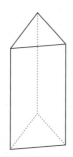

1. What is the shape of each face?
2. What is the shape of each base?

Need a little help? Check out Review It before moving on.

⟨**Ans.**⟩ 1. Rectangle   2. Triangle

Review It

The solids below are called **prisms**. The sides of a **prism** are made up of flat **faces**.

Triangular prism	Quadrangular prism	Pentagonal prism	Hexagonal prism
triangle	quadrilateral	pentagon	hexagon

In a **triangular prism**, each of the two **bases** are triangles. Both bases of a triangular prism are congruent.

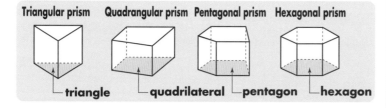

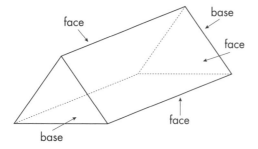

A **pyramid** is a solid whose base is polygonal and sides are all triangles.

The faces of all **pyramids** are triangles. A **regular pyramid** is the pyramid whose base is a regular polygon and whose sides are all congruent isosceles triangles.

Ex. In a **hexagonal pyramid**, the base is a hexagon.

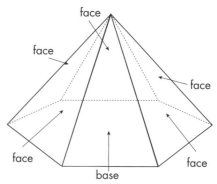

pp. 1–65
Algebra

pp. 67–151
Geometry

pp. 153–183
Probability & Statistics

pp. 185–197
Review

Practice It

1 **Answer each of the following questions about the hexagonal pyramid.**

10 points each

(1) What shape is each face?

⟨Ans.⟩ _____

(2) What shape is the base?

⟨Ans.⟩ _____

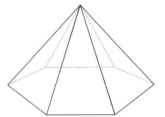

2 **Answer each of the following questions about the pentagonal prism.**

10 points each

(1) What shape is each face?

⟨Ans.⟩ _____

(2) How many faces are there?

⟨Ans.⟩ _____

(3) What shape is each base?

⟨Ans.⟩ _____

(4) How many bases are there?

⟨Ans.⟩ _____

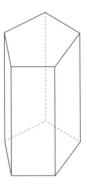

3 **Answer each of the following questions about the square pyramid.**

10 points each

(1) How many faces are there?

⟨Ans.⟩ _____

(2) How many bases are there?

⟨Ans.⟩ _____

(3) State all the edges that intersect *OBC*.

⟨Ans.⟩ _____

(4) State all the edges in a skewed position with $\overline{BC}$.

⟨Ans.⟩ _____

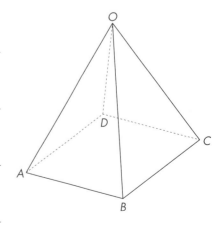

39 Solids and Nets 2

Geometry 13

Name

Date / /

Score /100

 Remember It

Give these problems a try.

For each of the following nets, draw the built shape.

1.

2.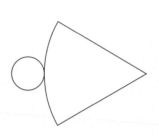

3.

Need a little help? Check out Review It before moving on.

(**Ans.**) 1.–3. See images in Review It.

 Review It

Remember that a **net** is a 2-dimensional shape that can be folded to form a 3-dimensional shape.

Ex. Rectangular prism

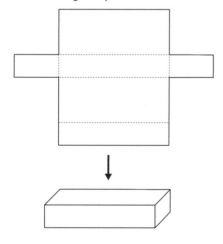

Ex. Cylinder

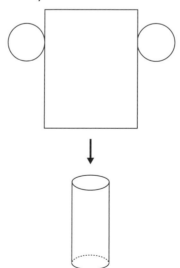

Ex. Cone

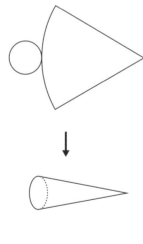

 © Kumon Publishing Co., Ltd.

Practice It

1 The net of a rectangular prism is shown. Use the net to answer each of the following questions.

20 points each

(1) State all surfaces parallel to *HIJK*.

⟨Ans.⟩ _____

(2) State all surfaces perpendicular to *HCDG*.

⟨Ans.⟩ _____

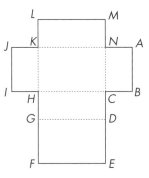

2 The net of a cube is shown. Use this figure to answer each of the following questions.

20 points each

(1) State all surfaces perpendicular to ⑤.

⟨Ans.⟩ _____

(2) State all surfaces that intersect to form $\overline{AB}$.

⟨Ans.⟩ _____

(3) State all surfaces parallel to ②.

⟨Ans.⟩ _____

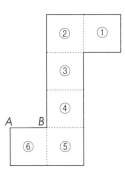

Name

Date

Score

/ 100

Remember It

Give these problems a try.

Answer each of the following questions about the triangular prism.

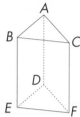

1. Plane *P* is parallel to *ABC* and *DEF* and cuts through the triangular prism. What is the shape of the cross-section?
2. Plane *Q* is parallel to *BCFE* and cuts through the triangular prism. What is the shape of the cross-section?

Need a little help? Check out Review It before moving on.

⟨Ans.⟩ **1.** Triangle   **2.** Rectangle

Review It

When cutting straight through an object, a **cross-section** is the resulting shape. It can also be thought of as the shape that is the result when a plane is intersecting a solid. The cross-section of any 3-dimensional solid is a 2-dimensional shape.

Ex. What is the shape of the cross-section that results from plane *P* intersecting with the triangular prism from Review It? → A triangular prism is made up of two triangle bases.
Since plane *P* is parallel to the base *DEF*, the cross-section is a triangle.

Ex. What is the shape of the cross-section that results from plane *Q* intersecting with the triangular prism from Review It? The triangular prism has rectangular faces.
Since plane *Q* is parallel to the face *BCFE*, the cross-section is a rectangle.

A solid with two circular bases is a **cylinder**. A **pyramid** has one base, which is a polygon.
A **cone** has one base, which is a circle. The sides of a cylinder and a cone are curved surfaces, not flat surfaces.

Ex. Plane *R* is parallel to the two bases and cuts through the cylinder.
What is the shape of the cross-section? → Circle

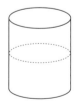

Ex. Plane *S* is perpendicular to the two bases and cuts through the cylinder.
What is the shape of the cross-section? → Rectangle

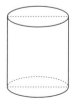

pp. 1–65
Algebra

pp. 67–151
Geometry

pp. 153–183
Probability & Statistics

pp. 185–197
Review

Practice It

1 **Answer each of the following questions about the cube.**

20 points each

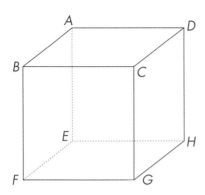

(1) Plane *J* is parallel to *BCGF* and cuts through the cube.
What is the shape of the cross-section?   〈Ans.〉 _____

(2) Plane *K* is parallel to *ABCD* and cuts through the cube.
What is the shape of the cross-section?   〈Ans.〉 _____

(3) Plane *L* is formed by the diagonals *BG* and *AH*. What is the shape of the cross-section
when plane *L* cuts through the cube?   〈Ans.〉 _____

2 **Answer each of the following questions about the square pyramid.**

20 points each

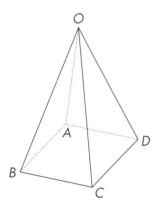

(1) Plane *M* is parallel to *ABCD* and cuts through the pyramid.
What is the shape of the cross-section?   〈Ans.〉 _____

(2) Plane *N* is created by $\overline{OD}$ and the diagonal *BD*. What is the shape of the cross-section
when plane *N* cuts through the pyramid?   〈Ans.〉 _____

© Kumon Publishing Co., Ltd.

Projection of a Solid

Name

Date   /   /

Score   / 100

 Remember It

Give these problems a try.

For each of the solids, draw the projections when viewed from the top and side of the figure.

1. Square pyramid

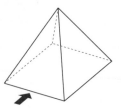

Top projection:

Side projection:

2. Cylinder

Top projection:

Side projection:

3. Cube

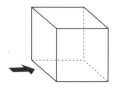

Top projection:

Side projection:

Need a little help? Check out Review It before moving on.

(**Ans.**) 1.–3. See images in Review It.

Review It

A **projection** is the shape of a solid, when viewed either directly above or directly from the side of the solid. The projection of any 3-dimensional solid is a 2-dimensional shape.

Ex. Draw the projections for a square pyramid, a cylinder, and a cube.

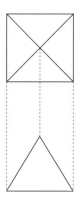
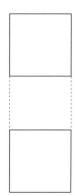
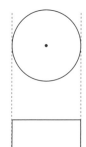

 © Kumon Publishing Co., Ltd.

Practice It

1 For each of the solids, draw the projections when viewed from the top and side of the figure.

(1)(2) 15 points each, (3) 20 points

(1) Cone	(2) Triangular prism	(3) Triangular pyramid
Projections	Projections	Projections
Top	Top	Top
Side	Side	Side

2 Draw the built shape shown by the projection and write its name.

(1)(2) 15 points each, (3) 20 points

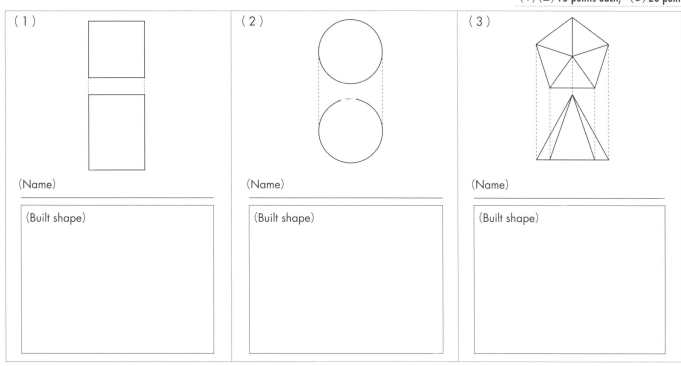

(1)	(2)	(3)
(Name)	(Name)	(Name)
(Built shape)	(Built shape)	(Built shape)

Volume and Surface Area
Solids and Spheres

Name _____

Date ___ / ___ / ___   Score ___ / 100

Remember It

Give these problems a try.

Find the volume of the following shapes.

1.

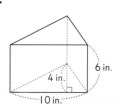

2.

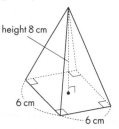

height 8 cm

6 cm

6 cm

Need a little help? Check out Review It before moving on.

⟨**Ans.**⟩ 1. 120 in.³   2. 96 cm³

Review It

Recall that the volume of any prism or any cylinder is calculated the same. The table below shows the volume formula for different figures.

Volume of prism or cylinder

$(V) =$ area of the base (B) × height (h)

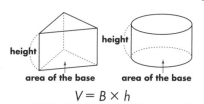

height   height

area of the base   area of the base

$$V = B \times h$$

Ex. Find the volume:

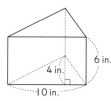

6 in.

4 in.

10 in.

Since the area of the triangular base is:

$\dfrac{1}{2} \times 10 \times 4 = 20$ in.² and the height is 6 in., the volume is:

$20 \times 6 = 120$ in.³

Volume of square pyramid or cone

$(V) = \dfrac{1}{3} \times$ area of the base (B) × height (h)

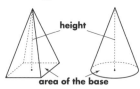

height

area of the base

$$V = \dfrac{1}{3}(B \times h)$$

Ex. Find the volume:

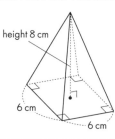

height 8 cm

6 cm

6 cm

Since the area of the square base is:

$6 \times 6 = 36$ cm² and the height is 8 cm, the volume is:

$\dfrac{1}{3}(36 \times 8) = 96$ cm³

Volume of sphere

$(V) = \dfrac{4}{3} \times$ [pi = π] × radius $(r)^3$

$$V = \dfrac{4}{3}\pi r^3$$

Surface area of sphere

$(S) = 4 \times$ [pi = π] × radius $(r)^2$

$$S = 4\pi r^2$$

Ex. Find the volume and surface area of the sphere. Use π in your answer.

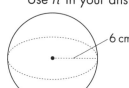

6 cm

$V = \dfrac{4}{3}\pi (6)^3 = 288\pi$ cm³

$S = 4\pi (6)^2 = 144\pi$ cm²

Practice It

1 **Find the volume of each of the following shapes.**

25 points each

(1)

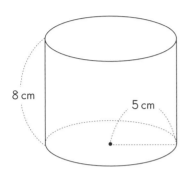

8 cm
5 cm

⟨**Ans.**⟩ _____

(2)

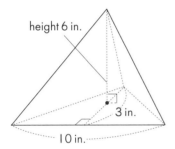

height 6 in.
3 in.
10 in.

⟨**Ans.**⟩ _____

2 **Find the volume and surface area of the sphere.**
Use π in your answer.

25 points each

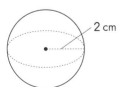

2 cm

⟨**Ans.**⟩ V = _____ , S = _____

Net and Surface Area
Prisms, Cylinders, Pyramids, and Cones

Name

Date   /   /

Score   / 100

Remember It

Give these problems a try.

Draw the shape of the solid whose net is shown below.

1.

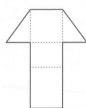

2.

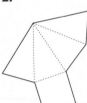

3.

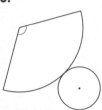

Need a little help? Check out Review It before moving on.

⟨**Ans.**⟩ 1.–3. See images in Review It.

Review It

A 2-dimensional net is created when we unfold a 3-dimensional shape.

Ex. Draw the shape of the solid whose net is shown.

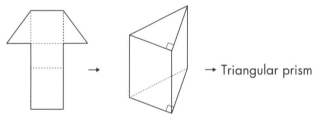

→ Triangular prism

Ex.

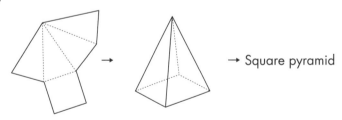

→ Square pyramid

Ex.

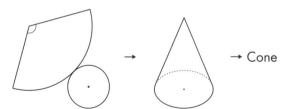

→ Cone

 © Kumon Publishing Co., Ltd.

Practice It

1 Draw the shape of the solid whose net is shown below.

15 points each

(1)

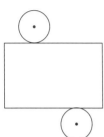

(2)

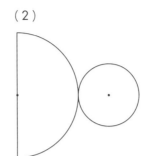

2 Find the surface area.

15 points each

(1)

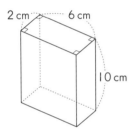

2 cm   6 cm

10 cm

The total area of both the top base and bottom base is

$12 + 12 =$ _____ cm² and the total area of the lateral faces is

$60 + 20 + 60 + 20 =$ _____ cm², so the total surface area is:

$24 + 160 =$ _____ cm²

(2)

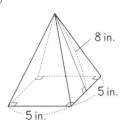

8 in.

5 in.

5 in.

The area of the base is _____ in.² and the total area of the lateral

faces is _____ in.², so the total surface area is: _____ in.²

3 Answer the following questions using the net shown.

20 points each

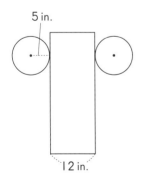

5 in.

12 in.

(1) Draw the shape of the solid.

(2) Find the surface area of the solid. Use π in your answer.

⟨Ans.⟩ _____

Geometry Quiz 2

Name

Date   /   /

Score   / 100

1   Plane *X* and plane *Y* are parallel. They both are perpendicular to line ℓ, as shown on the figure. Use this information to answer each of the questions below.   15 points each

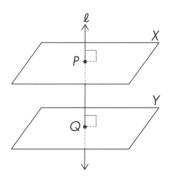

(1)   Line *m* is parallel to line ℓ. State the relationship between line *m* and plane *X*. Use the relevant mathematical symbol.

⟨**Ans.**⟩ _____

(2)   Line *n* is on plane *X*. State the relationship between line *n* and plane *Y*. Use the relevant mathematical symbol.

⟨**Ans.**⟩ _____

2   Draw the projection of the hexagonal prism when viewed from the side of the shape.   14 points

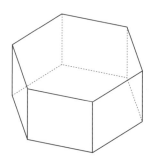

  © Kumon Publishing Co., Ltd.

3 The figures on the right show the net and the built shape of a rectangular prism. Use the figures to answer each of the following questions. 8 points each

(1) When assembling the net, which of the other vertices intersect with vertex *L*?

〈**Ans.**〉 _____

(2) When assembling the net, which of the other vertices intersect with vertex *H*?

〈**Ans.**〉 _____

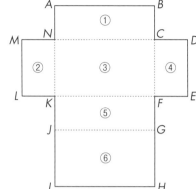

4 Answer the following questions, using the net shown. 10 points each

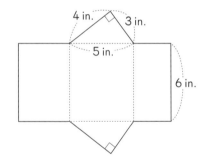

(1) Draw the shape of the solid.

(2) What is the area of the base?
  (a) 6 in.^{2} (b) 12 in.^{2} (c) 18 in.^{2} (d) 30 in.^{2}

(3) What is the surface area of the entire solid?
  (a) 78 in.^{2} (b) 84 in.^{2} (c) 90 in.^{2} (d) 96 in.^{2}

(4) What is the volume of the entire solid?
  (a) 30 in.^{3} (b) 36 in.^{3} (c) 60 in.^{3} (d) 72 in.^{3} (e) 120 in.^{3}

Parallel Lines and Angles

Name _____

Date ___ / ___ / ___   Score ___ / 100

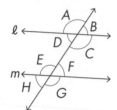

Remember It

Give these problems a try.

Use the figure below to answer the following questions, where line ℓ is parallel to line m.

1. Which angles are adjacent to $\angle C$?
2. Which angles are alternate interior angles?
3. Which angles are alternate exterior angles?

Need a little help? Check out Review It before moving on.

⟨Ans.⟩ 1. $\angle B$, $\angle D$ 2. $\angle C$ and $\angle E$, $\angle D$ and $\angle F$ 3. $\angle A$ and $\angle G$, $\angle B$ and $\angle H$

Review It

The angles created when dividing a line into two are the **adjacent angles**. Adjacent angles are supplementary.

Ex. Which angles are adjacent to $\angle C$?

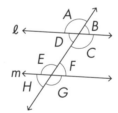

$\angle B$ and $\angle D$ are adjacent to $\angle C$.

A line passing through two lines is the **transversal**.
Alternate angles that lie on the inner side of the two lines are called **alternate interior angles**.

Ex. Which angles are alternate interior angles?

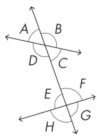

$\angle C$ and $\angle E$; $\angle D$ and $\angle F$ are alternate interior angles.

Alternate angles that lie on the outer side of the two lines are called **alternate exterior angles**.

Ex. Which angles are alternate exterior angles?
$\angle A$ and $\angle G$; $\angle B$ and $\angle H$ are alternate exterior angles.

    © Kumon Publishing Co., Ltd.

pp. 1–65
Algebra

pp. 67–151
Geometry

pp. 153–183
Probability & Statistics

pp. 185–197
Review

Practice It

1 Use the figure to determine if each of the following statements are true or
false. Write "T" for true and write "F" for false.   10 points each

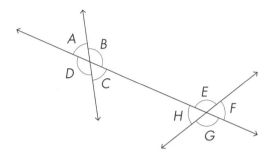

(1) ∠C ≅ ∠E   〈Ans.〉 _____   (2) ∠F ≅ ∠G   〈Ans.〉 _____

(3) ∠A ≅ ∠C   〈Ans.〉 _____   (4) ∠B ≅ ∠F   〈Ans.〉 _____

2 Use the figure below to answer each of the following questions, where line *m*
is parallel to line *n*, where m∠A = 35°.   10 points each

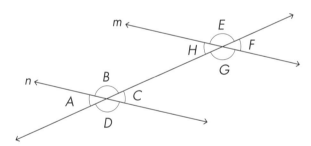

(1) What is the measurement of ∠C?   〈Ans.〉 _____

(2) What is the measurement of ∠D?   〈Ans.〉 _____

(3) What is the measurement of ∠F?   〈Ans.〉 _____

(4) What is the measurement of ∠H?   〈Ans.〉 _____

(5) What is the measurement of ∠G?   〈Ans.〉 _____

(6) If line *m* was not parallel to line *n*, would ∠C be congruent to ∠H?

            〈Ans.〉 _____

Opposite Angles and Opposite Sides

Name

Date ___ / ___ / ___

Score ___ / 100

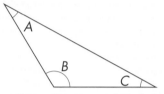

Remember It

Give these problems a try.

Answer the questions below about △ABC , where m∠A and m∠C are less than 90° and m∠B is greater than 90°.

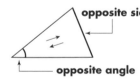

1. What is the opposite side of ∠B?
2. What angle is opposite $\overline{AB}$?
3. Is ∠C an acute angle, right angle, or obtuse angle?
4. Is ∠B an acute angle, right angle, or obtuse angle?

Need a little help? Check out Review It before moving on.

⟨Ans.⟩ 1. $\overline{AC}$ 2. ∠C   3. Acute angle   4. Obtuse angle

Review It

A triangle has three sides and three angles. There is an angle between each of the two sides. The side opposite of the angle is called the **opposite side**. Alternatively, the angle opposite of the side is called the **opposite angle**.

opposite side

opposite angle

Ex. What is the opposite side of ∠B in the triangle above? → $\overline{AC}$

Ex. What is the opposite angle of $\overline{AB}$ in the triangle above? → ∠C

A right triangle has one angle of 90°.

right triangle

An acute triangle has three angles less than 90°.

acute triangle

An obtuse triangle has one angle greater than 90°.

obtuse triangle

Ex. Is △ABC (above) an acute triangle, right triangle, or obtuse triangle? → Since △ABC has one obtuse angle, it is an obtuse triangle.

pp. 1–65
Algebra

pp. 67–151
Geometry

pp. 153–183
Probability & Statistics

pp. 185–197
Review

 Practice It

1 Answer the questions below about △**PQR**, where ∠**P** ≅ ∠**Q** and ∠**R** is an obtuse angle.

10 points each

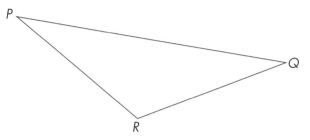

(1)   Is △PQR an acute triangle?   〈Ans.〉＿＿＿＿＿＿＿＿＿

(2)   Which side is the longest?   In a triangle, the longest side is   〈Ans.〉＿＿＿＿＿＿＿＿＿
                                    opposite to the largest angle.

(3)   What is the relationship between $\overline{PR}$ and $\overline{QR}$?

                                                             〈Ans.〉＿＿＿＿＿＿＿＿＿

(4)   If $m\angle R = 110°$, what is the measurement of ∠Q?   〈Ans.〉＿＿＿＿＿＿＿＿＿

2 Answer the questions about △**ABC**, where $m\angle C = 40°$ and ∠**B** is a right angle.

12 points each

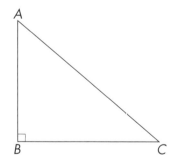

(1)   What is the measurement of ∠B?   〈Ans.〉＿＿＿＿＿＿＿＿＿

(2)   What is the measurement of ∠A?   〈Ans.〉＿＿＿＿＿＿＿＿＿

(3)   Is △ABC an acute triangle, right triangle, or obtuse triangle?   〈Ans.〉＿＿＿＿＿＿＿＿＿

(4)   Which side is the largest side?   〈Ans.〉＿＿＿＿＿＿＿＿＿

(5)   Which side is the shortest side?   〈Ans.〉＿＿＿＿＿＿＿＿＿

Remember It

Give these problems a try.

Use the figure to answer each of the following questions.

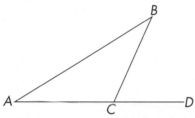

1.   Identify the exterior angle in the figure.
2.   If $m\angle A = 40°$ and $m\angle B = 30°$, what is $m\angle BCD$?

Need a little help? Check out Review It before moving on.

⟨Ans.⟩ 1. ∠BCD   2. 70°

Review It

For every triangle, the angle that is formed when extending a side at any vertex is called an **exterior angle**.

Ex. Identify the exterior angle in the figure above. → Since $\overline{BC}$ is extended, $\angle BCD$ is an exterior angle.

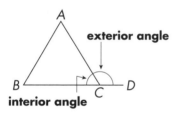

The measurement of any exterior angle is equal to the sum of the two interior angles not next to the exterior angle.

Ex. If $m\angle A = 40°$ and $m\angle B = 30°$, what is $m\angle BCD$? → $m\angle BCD = m\angle A + m\angle B = 70°$

The **sum of all three interior angles of a triangle is 180°.**

Ex. What is $m\angle C$? → $m\angle A + m\angle B + m\angle C = 180°$
$$70 + m\angle C = 180°$$
$$m\angle C = 110°$$

Practice It

1 **Use the figure to answer each of the following questions.**   10 points each

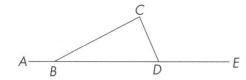

(1) Identify all the interior angles and exterior angles of △CBD.

Interior angles: _____

Exterior angles: _____

(2) The sum of the measurements of ∠BCD and ∠CDB is congruent to
the measurement of which angle?   ⟨Ans.⟩ _____

(3) What is the sum of the measurements of ∠CBD, ∠BCD, and ∠BDC?   ⟨Ans.⟩ _____

2 **Use the figure to answer each of the following questions, where _m∠ABC_ = 51°
and ∠CAB is a right angle.**   10 points each

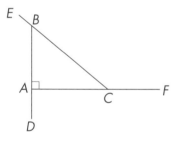

(1) What is the measurement of ∠BCF?   ⟨Ans.⟩ _____

(2) What is the measurement of ∠CAD?   ⟨Ans.⟩ _____

(3) What is the measurement of ∠EBD?   ⟨Ans.⟩ _____

(4) What is the sum of the measurements of all three exterior angles?   ⟨Ans.⟩ _____

3 **Find the measurement of ∠x in the figure below.**   20 points

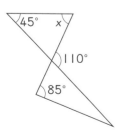

⟨Ans.⟩ _____

Remember It

Give these problems a try.

Given the pentagon. Answer each of the following questions, using the figure.

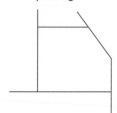

1. What is the sum of all the interior angles of the pentagon?
2. What is the sum of all the exterior angles of the pentagon?

Need a little help? Check out Review It before moving on.

⟨Ans.⟩ 1. 540°   2. 360°

Review It

The formula of the **sum of the interior angles of a polygon with an *n* angles** is: $180° \times (n - 2)$.
The **sum of all exterior angles in a polygon** is 360°.

Ex. What is the sum of all the interior angles of a pentagon?
$n = 5 \rightarrow 180 \times (5 - 2) = 180 \times 3 = 540°$

Ex. What is the sum of all the interior angles of a hexagon?
$n = 6 \rightarrow 180 \times (6 - 2) = 180 \times 4 = 720°$

Remember that a **regular polygon** is a polygon whose sides are all congruent. The interior angles of a regular polygon are also all congruent.

Practice It

1 **List the number of sides, *n*, of each of the following polygons.**   10 points each

(1) Pentagon: $n =$ _____   (2) Hexagon: $n =$ _____

(3) Octagon: $n =$ _____   (4) Nonagon: $n =$ _____

(5) Decagon: $n =$ _____   (6) Dodecagon: $n =$ _____

2 **State the sum of all the interior angles for each of the following polygons.**

10 points each

(1) Dodecagon ⟨**Ans.**⟩ _____

(2) Octagon ⟨**Ans.**⟩ _____

3 **Find the measurement of ∠x in each of the following figures.** 10 points each

(1)

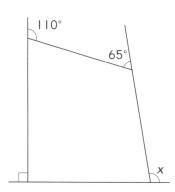

⟨**Ans.**⟩ _____

(2)

⟨**Ans.**⟩ _____

Remember It

Give these problems a try.

Given circles *O*, *P*, and *Q*. Use the figures to answer each of the following questions.

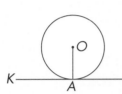 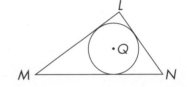

1. If $\overline{OA}$ and $\overline{KA}$ touch at only one point, what is the relationship between $\overline{OA}$ and $\overline{KA}$?
2. Fill in each of the following boxes by writing either "circumscribed" or "inscribed."
   - Triangle *GHI* is a(n) [_____] triangle and circle *P* is a(n) [_____] circle.
   - Triangle *LMN* is a(n) [_____] triangle and circle *Q* is a(n) [_____] circle.

Need a little help? Check out Review It before moving on.

⟨**Ans.**⟩ **1.** $\overline{OA} \perp \overline{KA}$ **2.** inscribed, circumscribed; circumscribed, inscribed

 Review It

If two circles or a circle and a straight line that touch but do not cross, they are **tangent** to each other. A straight line that touches a curve or a circle is called a **tangent (line)**.

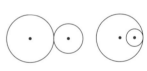

When there is only one intersection point between a circle and a line, the line is tangent to the circle, and creates a right angle with the radius.

Ex. What is the relationship between $\overline{OA}$ and $\overline{KA}$ above? → $\overline{OA}$ is perpendicular to $\overline{KA}$.

When one shape is inside another shape, the inner shape is **inscribed** and the outer shape is **circumscribed**.

Ex. In the figures above, identify a shape that is circumscribed and a shape that is inscribed. → Triangle *GHI* is inscribed in circle *P*, while triangle *LMN* circumscribes circle *Q*.

The measurement of any inscribed angle is $\frac{1}{2}$ the measurement of its corresponding central angle.

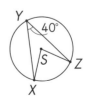

Ex. Given the figure below, where $m\angle XYZ = 40°$. Find $m\angle XSZ$.

The measurement of $\angle XSZ$ is double the measurement of $\angle XYZ$, so $m\angle XSZ = 80°$.

pp. 1–65
Algebra

pp. 67–151
Geometry

pp. 153–183
Probability & Statistics

pp. 185–197
Review

Ex. If the measurement of ∠XYZ was doubled, how would the measurement of ∠XSZ change?

The measurement of inscribed angle ∠XYZ is $\frac{1}{2}$ the measurement of the central angle ∠XSZ, so if the measurement of ∠XYZ was doubled, then the measurement of ∠XSZ would also double.

Practice It

1 **Find the measurement of ∠x in each of the following figures.**   10 points each

(1)

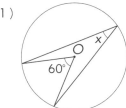

⟨Ans.⟩ _____

(2)

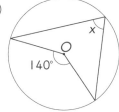

⟨Ans.⟩ _____

(3)

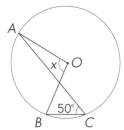

⟨Ans.⟩ _____

2 **Given the figure, where m∠ABD = 50°. Use the figure to answer each of the following questions.**   15 points each

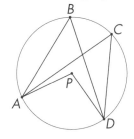

(1) Find m∠APD.

⟨Ans.⟩ _____

(2) Find m∠ACD.

⟨Ans.⟩ _____

3 **Find the measurement of ∠y in the figure below.**   20 points

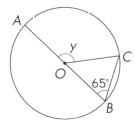

⟨Ans.⟩ _____

4 **Find the measurement of ⌢BC in the figure below.**   20 points

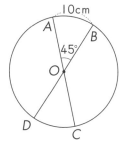

⟨Ans.⟩ _____

Geometry Quiz 3

Name

_____

Date   Score

___ / ___ / ___   _____ / 100

1 Find the measurement of the missing angles in the figure below, where line ℓ is parallel to line *m*.   10 points each

(1)

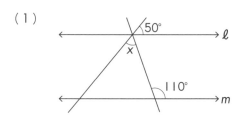

⟨**Ans.**⟩ $m\angle x =$ _____

(2)

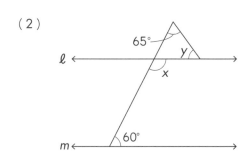

⟨**Ans.**⟩ $m\angle x =$ _____ , $m\angle y =$ _____

2 Use the figure on the right to answer each of the following questions, where $m\angle ABC = 125°$ and $m\angle CAB = 20°$.   8 points each

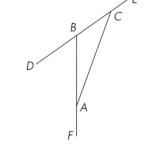

(1) What is the measurement of $\angle ACE$?

⟨**Ans.**⟩ _____

(2) Is △ABC an acute triangle, a right triangle, or an obtuse triangle?

⟨**Ans.**⟩ _____

(3) Which side of △ABC is the longest side?

⟨**Ans.**⟩ _____

(4) Which side of △ABC is the shortest side?

⟨**Ans.**⟩ _____

    © *Kumon Publishing Co., Ltd.*

3 **Find the measurement of the missing angles in the figure below.**   10 points each

(1)

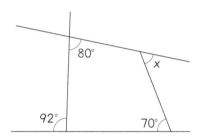

⟨**Ans.**⟩ $m\angle x =$ _____ , $m\angle y =$ _____

(2)

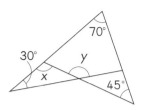

⟨**Ans.**⟩ $m\angle x =$ _____

(3)

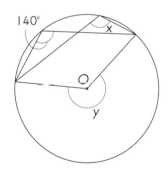

⟨**Ans.**⟩ $m\angle x =$ _____

4 **Use the figure to answer each of the following questions.**   9 points each

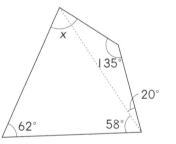

(1)   What is the measurement of $\angle x$?

   (a) 40°   (b) 70°   (c) 80°   (d) 140°   (e) 280°

(2)   What is the measurement of $\angle y$?

   (a) 40°   (b) 70°   (c) 80°   (d) 140°   (e) 280°

Name

Date

Score

/ /   / 100

Remember It

Give these problems a try.

In the figure, *ABCD* and *PQRS* are congruent. Use the figure to answer each of the following questions.

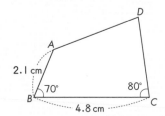
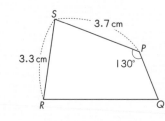

1. Which side corresponds to $\overline{AB}$?
2. What is the measurement of $\overline{PQ}$?
3. What is the measurement of ∠*R*?

Need a little help? Check out Review It before moving on.

(Ans.) 1. $\overline{PQ}$ 2. 2.1 cm   3. 80°

Review It

Two plane figures are **congruent** when they have the same size and shape. In congruent figures, **corresponding sides**, **vertices**, and **angles** are congruent. When one figure can perfectly overlap with another figure, they are congruent.

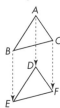

$\triangle ABC \cong \triangle DEF$

Ex. $\overline{AB} = 2.1$ cm, so $\overline{PQ} = 2.1$ cm.

In congruent figures, corresponding angles are congruent.

Ex. $m\angle C = 80°$, so $m\angle R = 80°$.

For congruent triangles, the measure of three angles and the lengths of three sides are all congruent. If the following conditions are true, the triangles are congruent:

① The lengths of three corresponding sides are congruent.
② The lengths of two corresponding sides and the measures of the included angles are congruent.
③ The measures of two corresponding angles and the length of the included sides are congruent.

① **Side-Side-Side (SSS)**   ② **Side-Angle-Side (SAS)**   ③ **Angle-Side-Angle (ASA)**

Ex. In the figures, $\overline{AB}$ is congruent to $\overline{DE}$. Show that $\triangle ABC$ is congruent to $\triangle DEF$.

① $\overline{AB} \cong \overline{DE}$, $\overline{BC} \cong \overline{EF}$, $\overline{AC} \cong \overline{DF}$
② $\overline{AB} \cong \overline{DE}$, $\angle A \cong \angle D$, $\overline{AC} \cong \overline{DF}$ or
   $\overline{AB} \cong \overline{DE}$, $\angle B \cong \angle E$, $\overline{BC} \cong \overline{EF}$
③ $\overline{AB} \cong \overline{DE}$, $\angle A \cong \angle D$, $\angle B \cong \angle E$

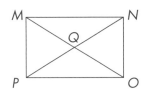

Practice It

1 In the figure, rectangle *MNOP* is divided by its two diagonals. Use the figure to answer each of the following questions.

10 points each

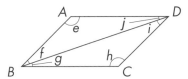

(1) Which triangle(s) is/are congruent to △*MQP*?
Since congruent figures have congruent corresponding sides and congruent corresponding angles, △*MQP* is congruent to _____.

(2) Which triangle(s) is/are congruent to △*NOP*?

> Congruent figures can completely overlap each other when moving or turning over.

Since congruent triangles have congruent, corresponding sides and congruent, corresponding angles, △*NOP* is congruent to _____, _____, and _____.

2 In the figure, two triangles are formed by the diagonal of parallelogram *ABCD*. Use this figure to answer each of the following questions.

10 points each

(1) Which side corresponds to $\overline{AB}$? ⟨Ans.⟩ _____

(2) Which angle corresponds to ∠*j*? ⟨Ans.⟩ _____

3 Given a triangle, where $\overline{AB} \cong \overline{AC}$, *M* is the midpoint of *BC*, and ∠*ABM* ≅ ∠*ACM*. Use the information to answer each of the following questions.

10 points each

(1) Given *M* is the midpoint of $\overline{BC}$, which two line segments are congruent?
⟨Ans.⟩ _____

(2) Which of the methods is easiest to show △*AMB* ≅ △*AMC*?

Side-Side-Side (SSS)   Side-Angle-Side (SAS)   Angle-Side-Angle (ASA)
⟨Ans.⟩ _____

4 Given the circle, where $\overline{AC}$ and $\overline{BD}$ are both diameters. Prove that △*AOB* ≅ △*COD* by completing the following steps.

10 points each

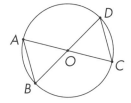

(1) Step 1: Point *O* is the midpoint of $\overline{AC}$, so _____ ≅ _____.

(2) Step 2: Point *O* is the midpoint of $\overline{BD}$, so _____.

(3) Step 3: ∠*AOB* and ∠*COD* are vertical angles, so _____.

(4) Conclusion: By the _____ Method, △*AOB* ≅ △*COD*.

Name _____

Date ____ / ____ / ____   Score _____ / 100

 Remember It

Give these problems a try.

Given the figure of △ABC, where △ABC is an isosceles triangle, AM is the angle bisector of ∠BAC, and BC is not congruent to either $\overline{AB}$ or $\overline{AC}$. Use this figure to answer each of the following questions.

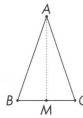

1. State which sides of △ABC are congruent.
2. State which angles of △ABC are congruent.
3. State the relationship between $\overline{BM}$ and $\overline{CM}$, and the relationship between $\overline{AM}$ and $\overline{BC}$. Use the correct mathematical symbol.

Need a little help? Check out Review It before moving on.

⟨Ans.⟩ 1. $\overline{AC} \cong \overline{AB}$ 2. ∠B ≅ ∠C   3. $\overline{BM} \cong \overline{CM}$ and $\overline{AM} \perp \overline{BC}$

 Review It

Properties of an Isosceles Triangle
① Two sides of an isosceles triangle are congruent.
② The base angles of an isosceles triangle are congruent.
③ The bisector of the vertex angle bisects the base perpendicularly in an isosceles triangle.

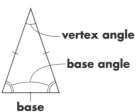

vertex angle
base angle
base

① **Ex.** Which sides of △ABC above, are congruent?
  → $\overline{BC}$ is not congruent to either $\overline{AB}$ or $\overline{AC}$, so $\overline{AC} \cong \overline{AB}$.

② **Ex.** Which angles of △ABC are congruent?
  → ∠B ≅ ∠C.

③ **Ex.** What is the relationship between $\overline{BM}$ and $\overline{CM}$, and between $\overline{AM}$ and $\overline{BC}$?
  → $\overline{BM} \cong \overline{CM}$ and $\overline{AM} \perp \overline{BC}$.

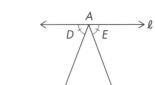 **Practice It**

1 **Given the figure, where line ℓ is parallel to line m and ∠D ≅ ∠E. Prove that △ABC is an isosceles triangle by completing each of the following steps.**

5 points each

(1) Step 1: Since ℓ ∥ m, so ∠D ≅ _____.
(2) Step 2: Since ℓ ∥ m, so ∠E ≅ _____.
(3) Step 3: Since ∠D ≅ ∠E, so ∠G ≅ _____.
(4) Conclusion: Since ∠G ≅ ∠H, so △ABC is a(n) _____ triangle.

2 Given the figure, where $\overline{AB} \cong \overline{AC}$ and $\overline{DB} \cong \overline{CE}$. Prove that $\triangle ADE$ is an isosceles triangle by completing each of the following steps.   8 points each

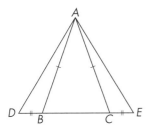

(1) Step 1: Since $\overline{AB} \cong \overline{AC}$, so $\triangle ABC$ is a(n) _____ triangle.

(2) Step 2: Since $\triangle ABC$ is an isosceles triangle, so $\angle ABC \cong$ _____.

(3) Step 3: Since the supplementary angle of $\angle ABC$ is _____, so $\angle ABD \cong$ _____.

(4) Step 4: By the Side-Angle-Side (SAS) Method, so $\triangle ABD \cong$ _____.

(5) Step 5: Since the two triangles are congruent, so $\overline{AD} \cong$ _____.

(6) Conclusion: Since $\overline{AD} \cong \overline{AE}$, so $\triangle ADE$ is a(n) _____ triangle.

3 Given $\triangle ABC$, where all the angles are congruent. Using the properties of isosceles triangles, show that the triangle is an equilateral triangle by completing each of the following steps.   8 points each

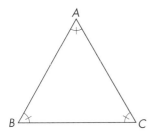

> If any two angles of a triangle are congruent, the triangle is an isosceles triangle. If all angles are congruent, the triangle is also an equilateral triangle.

(1) Step 1: Since $\angle B \cong \angle C$, $\triangle ABC$ is a(n) _____ triangle.

(2) Step 2: $\triangle ABC$ is an isosceles triangle, $\overline{AB} \cong$ _____.

(3) Step 3: Since $\angle A \cong \angle B$, by the same logic above, $\overline{BC} \cong$ _____.

(4) Conclusion: Since $\overline{AB} \cong \overline{BC} \cong \overline{AC}$, $\triangle ABC$ is a(n) _____ triangle.

Name

Date   /   /   Score   / 100

Remember It

Give these problems a try.

Given △PQR, where △PQR is an equilateral triangle. Use this information to answer each of the following questions.

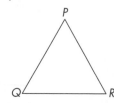

1. State which sides are congruent.
2. State which angles are congruent.
3. State the measurement of ∠Q.

Need a little help? Check out Review It before moving on.

⟨Ans.⟩ 1. $\overline{PQ} \cong \overline{QR} \cong \overline{RP}$ 2. $\angle P \cong \angle Q \cong \angle R$ 3. 60°

Review It

Properties of an Equilateral Triangle
① The three sides of an equilateral triangle are congruent.
② The three angles of an equilateral triangle are all congruent and measure 60°.
③ Since an equilateral triangle is a special form of an isosceles triangle, all the properties of an isosceles triangle apply.

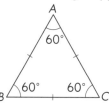

① **Ex.** Which sides of the equilateral triangle PQR are congruent? → $\overline{PQ} \cong \overline{QR} \cong \overline{RP}$.

Recall that the sum of all the interior angles of every triangle add up to 180°, so all of the interior angles in an equilateral triangle are congruent and always measure 60°.

② **Ex.** Which angles of the equilateral triangle PQR are congruent? → $\angle P \cong \angle Q \cong \angle R$.

③ **Ex.** What is the measurement of ∠Q in the equilateral triangle PQR? → $m\angle Q = 60°$.

Practice It

1. **An angle bisector is drawn at each of the vertices of equilateral triangle ABC. Describe the relationship between each angle bisector and its corresponding base. Use the correct mathematical symbol.**

10 points

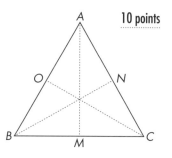

⟨Ans.⟩ _____ , _____ , and _____

2 In the equilateral triangle *FGH*, $\overline{FG}$ = 6 cm. Use this information to answer each of the following questions.　　10 points each

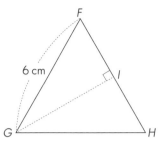

(1) What is the measurement of $\overline{FH}$?　　〈Ans.〉＿＿＿＿＿＿

(2) What is the measurement of $\overline{IH}$?　　〈Ans.〉＿＿＿＿＿＿

(3) What is the measurement of ∠*FGI*?　　〈Ans.〉＿＿＿＿＿＿

3 Given the figure where △*ABC* is an equilateral triangle and $\overline{AE} \cong \overline{BF} \cong \overline{CD}$. Prove that △*DEF* is an equilateral triangle by completing each of the following steps.　　12 points each

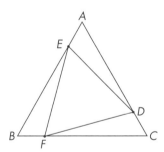

(1) Step 1: Since △*ABC* is an equilateral triangle, $\overline{AB} \cong$ ＿＿＿＿ $\cong$ ＿＿＿＿.

(2) Step 2: $\overline{AB} \cong \overline{BC} \cong \overline{CA}$ and $\overline{AE} \cong \overline{BF} \cong \overline{CD}$, $\overline{EB} \cong$ ＿＿＿＿ $\cong \overline{DA}$.

(3) Step 3: Since $\overline{AE} \cong \overline{BF} \cong \overline{CD}$, use the ＿＿＿＿＿＿＿＿＿ Method to conclude that △*AED* ≅ △*BFE* ≅ △*CDF*.

(4) Step 4: Since △*AED* ≅ △*BFE* ≅ △*CDF*, $\overline{EF} \cong$ ＿＿＿＿ $\cong$ ＿＿＿＿.

(5) Conclusion: $\overline{EF} \cong \overline{FD} \cong \overline{DE}$, therefore △*DEF* is a(n) ＿＿＿＿＿＿＿ triangle.

Name _____

Date _____ / _____ / _____   Score _____ / 100

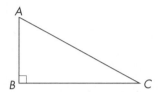 **Remember It**

Give these problems a try.

Given △ABC, where △ABC is a right triangle. Use the figure to answer each of the following questions.

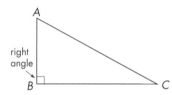

1. What is the measurement of ∠B?
2. Which side is the hypotenuse?

Need a little help? Check out Review It before moving on.

⟨Ans.⟩ 1. 90°   2. AC̄

 Review It

Recall that a **right angle** measures 90° and a triangle with a right angle is called a **right triangle**.

Ex. What is the measurement of ∠B in triangle ABC above? → ∠B is a right angle that measures 90°.

The **hypotenuse** of a right triangle is always the opposite side of the right angle. The hypotenuse is the longest side of a right triangle.

Ex. Which side of triangle ABC above is the hypotenuse? → The hypotenuse is the side opposite ∠B : AC̄.

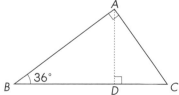 **Practice It**

1 Given △ABC, where △ABC is a right triangle, AD̄ ⊥ BC̄, and m∠B = 36°.
Use this information to answer each of the following questions.   8 points each

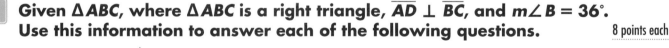

(1) What is the measurement of ∠BAD? 〈Ans.〉 _____

(2) What is the measurement of ∠DAC? 〈Ans.〉 _____

(3) What is the measurement of ∠ACD? 〈Ans.〉 _____

(4) How many hypotenuses are there? 〈Ans.〉 _____

Remember that a hypotenuse only applies to right triangles!

2 Given △**PQR**, where △**PQR** is a right triangle and is also an isosceles triangle (also known as an isosceles right triangle), where **PX** is the angle bisector of ∠**QPR**. Use this information to answer each of the following questions.

8 points each

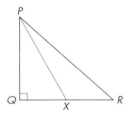

(1) What is the measurement of ∠QPR? 〈Ans.〉 _____

(2) What is the measurement of ∠QPX? 〈Ans.〉 _____

(3) What is the measurement of ∠PXR? 〈Ans.〉 _____

(4) What is the measurement of ∠PXQ? 〈Ans.〉 _____

3 Given △**ABC**, where $\overline{AB} \cong \overline{AC}$ and $\overline{AD}$ is the angle bisector of ∠**BAC**. Using the properties of a right triangle, show that △**ADB** ≅ △**ADC** by completing each of the following steps.

9 points each

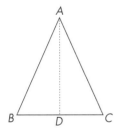

(1) Step 1: Since $\overline{AD}$ is the angle bisector of ∠BAC, so ∠BAD ≅ _____.

(2) Step 2: Since $\overline{AD}$ is the angle bisector of the vertex of △ABC, where △ABC is an isosceles triangle, so $\overline{AD} \perp$ _____.

(3) Step 3: Since $\overline{AD} \perp \overline{BC}$, so _____ = ☐°.

(4) Conclusion: Since $\overline{AD} \cong \overline{AD}$, so we can use the _____ Method to conclude that △ADB ≅ △ADC.

Name

Date

Score

/ /

/100

Remember It

Give these problems a try.

Given parallelogram *ABCD*. Use the figure to answer each of the following questions.

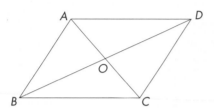

1. State which sides are parallel.
2. If $\overline{AB}$ is 6 cm, what is $\overline{CD}$?
3. Which angle is congruent to ∠*BAD*?
4. Which angle is congruent to ∠*ABC*?
5. State the relationship between $\overline{OB}$ and $\overline{OD}$ and the relationship between $\overline{AO}$ and $\overline{CO}$. Use the correct mathematical symbol.
6. What is the sum of the measurements of ∠*ABC* and ∠*BCD*?

Need a little help? Check out Review It before moving on.

⟨Ans.⟩ 1. $\overline{BC}$ and $\overline{AD}$ ∥ $\overline{DC}$ ∥ $\overline{AB}$ 2. 6 cm 3. ∠*DCB* 4. ∠*CDA* 5. $\overline{OB} \cong \overline{OD}$, $\overline{AO} \cong \overline{CO}$ 6. 180°

Review It

Recall that a parallelogram has two pairs of parallel, congruent sides.

   Ex. In *ABCD* above, $\overline{AD}$ ∥ $\overline{BC}$ and $\overline{AB}$ ∥ $\overline{DC}$ and $\overline{AD} \cong \overline{BC}$ and $\overline{AB} \cong \overline{DC}$.

The opposite angles of a parallelogram are congruent.

   Ex. ∠*BAD* ≅ ∠*DCB* and ∠*ABC* ≅ ∠*CDA*.

The two diagonals of a parallelogram bisect each other.

   Ex. $\overline{OB} \cong \overline{OD}$ and $\overline{AO} \cong \overline{CO}$.

The sum of two adjacent angles of a parallelogram is 180°.

   Ex. $m\angle ABC + m\angle BCD = 180°$.

Practice It

1 Given parallelogram *FGHI*, where m∠*GFH* = 50°, m∠*IFH* = 30° and
m∠*FGH* = 100°. Use the figure to answer each of the following problems.

10 points each

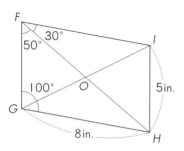

(1) Find $\overline{FI}$. ⟨Ans.⟩ _____

(2) Find m∠*HIF*. ⟨Ans.⟩ _____

(3) Find m∠*GHI*. ⟨Ans.⟩ _____

(4) If $\overline{FH}$ = 10 in., what is $\overline{OH}$? ⟨Ans.⟩ _____

2 Given that quadrilateral *XYZW* is a parallelogram.
Prove that △*XOW* ≅ △*ZOY* by completing each of the following steps. 15 points each

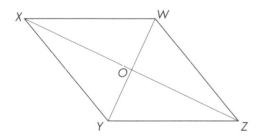

(1) Step 1: Since quadrilateral *XYZW* is a parallelogram, $\overline{XO}$ ≅ _____.

(2) Step 2: Since quadrilateral *XYZW* is a parallelogram, $\overline{WO}$ ≅ _____.

(3) Step 3: Using the property of vertical angles, ∠*XOW* ≅ _____.

(4) Conclusion: Using the _____ Method, △*XOW* ≅ △*ZOY*.

Name _____

Date _____ / _____ / _____   Score _____ / 100

 Remember It

Give these problems a try.

Given rectangle ABCD, where m∠DAC = 35°. Use this information to answer each of the following questions.

1. What is the measurement of ∠ABC?
2. What is the measurement of ∠BAC?
3. What is the measurement of ∠ACB?
4. If $\overline{AC}$ is 7 mm, what is the measurement of $\overline{BD}$?
5. If $\overline{AB}$ is 3 mm, what is the measurement of $\overline{DC}$?

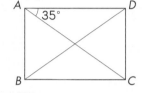

Need a little help? Check out Review It before moving on.

⟨Ans.⟩ 1. 90°   2. 55°   3. 35°   4. 7 mm   5. 3 mm

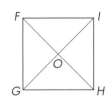 **Review It**

Recall that a **rectangle** is a parallelogram with four right angles.

Ex. In ABCD above, m∠ABC = 90° = m∠BAD, so m∠BAC = 90° − 35° = 55°.

Recall that the property of alternate angles, ∠DAC ≅ ∠ACB.

Since the diagonals of a rectangle are congruent, therefore $\overline{BD}$ = 7 mm.

Since a rectangle is a parallelogram with two pairs of parallel, congruent sides, so $\overline{AB} ≅ \overline{DC}$. Thus, $\overline{DC}$ is 3 mm.

Recall that a square is a rectangle. In a square, all four angles are right angles. However, the diagonals of a square are angle bisectors and perpendicular to each other.

Ex. Given square FGHI. Use this information to answer each of the following questions.

1. What is the measurement of ∠GHI? → All the angles are right angles. So, m∠GHI = 90°.

2. What is the measurement of ∠GHF? → m∠GHF = $\frac{90}{2}$ = 45°.

3. If $\overline{FG}$ is 14 mm, what is $\overline{GH}$? → $\overline{FG} = \overline{GH}$ = 14 mm.

4. What is the measurement of ∠FOI? → m∠FOI = 90°.

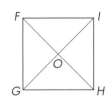

Practice It

1 **Given rectangle *ABCD*. Prove that Δ*ABD* ≅ Δ*CDB* by completing each of the following steps.**

9 points each

(1)   Step 1: Since a rectangle has four right angles, therefore $m\angle A \cong m\angle C =$ ▢°.

(2)   Step 2: Since a rectangle has two pairs of parallel, congruent sides, therefore $\overline{AB} \cong$ _____.

(3)   Step 3: Using the property of alternate angles, therefore $\angle ABD \cong$ _____.

(4)   Conclusion: Using the _____ Method, therefore Δ*ABD* ≅ Δ*CDB*.

2 **Quadrilateral *JKLM* is formed by the midpoints of the sides of square *FGHI*. Prove that *JKLM* is also a square, by completing each of the following steps.**

8 points each

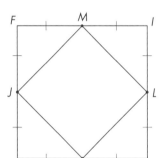

(1)   Step 1: Since *FGHI* is a square, therefore $m\angle F \cong m\angle G \cong m\angle H \cong m\angle I =$ ▢°.

(2)   Step 2: By the _____ Method, Δ*MFJ* ≅ Δ*JGK* ≅ Δ*KHL* ≅ Δ*LIM*.

(3)   Step 3: Using the properties of congruent triangles, therefore $\overline{MJ} \cong \overline{JK} \cong$ _____.

(4)   Step 4: Since Δ*FMJ* is a(n) _____ triangle,

  therefore $m\angle FJM \cong m\angle FMJ =$ ▢°.

(5)   Step 5: Using the same logic as in Step 4, therefore $m\angle GJK =$ ▢°.

(6)   Step 6: Using the property of straight angles, therefore $m\angle MJK =$ ▢°.

(7)   Step 7: Using the same logic as in Step 6, therefore $m\angle JKL \cong m\angle KLM \cong m\angle LMJ =$ ▢°.

(8)   Conclusion: Since quadrilateral *JKLM* has four congruent sides with four right angles, therefore

  quadrilateral *JKLM* is a(n) _____.

Name

Date   /   /   Score   / 100

Remember It

Give these problems a try.

Given rhombus $ABCD$, where $\overline{AB} = 4$ inches. Use this information to answer each of the following questions.

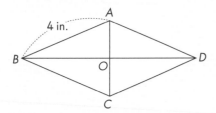

1. What is the length of $\overline{BC}$?
2. What is $m\angle BOA$?
3. What is the relationship between $\overline{AO}$ and $\overline{OC}$? Use the correct mathematical symbol.

Need a little help? Check out Review It before moving on.

⟨Ans.⟩ 1. 4 in.   2. 90°   3. $\overline{AO} \cong \overline{OC}$

Review It

1. Since a **rhombus** is a parallelogram with four congruent sides, therefore the measurement of $\overline{BC}$ is also 4 in.

2. Since the diagonals of a rhombus intersect perpendicularly, therefore the measurement of $\angle BOA$ is 90°.

3. Since a rhombus is a parallelogram, the two diagonals of a rhombus bisect each other. Thus, $\overline{AO} \cong \overline{OC}$.

Since a rhombus is a parallelogram with four congruent sides and all parallelograms are quadrilaterals, therefore a rhombus is also a parallelogram and a quadrilateral.

A rhombus can sometimes be a square, but not always. Likewise, a rhombus can sometimes be a rectangle, but not always.

Practice It

1 Given rhombus *FGHI*. Prove that △*GFO* ≅ △*IHO* by completing each of the following steps.

5 points each

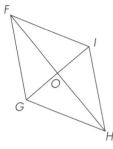

(1) Step 1: Since rhombus *FGHI* is a parallelogram, $\overline{GO}$ ≅ _____.

(2) Step 2: Since rhombus *FGHI* is a parallelogram, $\overline{FO}$ ≅ _____.

(3) Step 3: Since a rhombus has four congruent sides, $\overline{FG}$ ≅ _____.

(4) Conclusion: Using the _____ Method, △*GFO* ≅ △*IHO*.

2 Given rhombus *LMNO*, where $\overline{LX} \perp \overline{MN}$ and $\overline{LY} \perp \overline{NO}$.
Prove that $\overline{MX} \cong \overline{OY}$ by completing each of the following steps.

8 points each

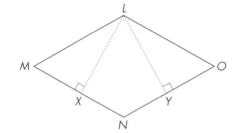

(1) Step 1: Since rhombus *LMNO* is a parallelogram,
∠*M* ≅ _____.

(2) Step 2: Since $\overline{LX} \perp \overline{MN}$ and $\overline{LY} \perp \overline{NO}$, ∠*LXM* ≅ _____.

(3) Step 3: Since ∠*LXM* ≅ ∠*LYO*, ∠*MLX* ≅ _____.

(4) Step 4: Since *LMNO* is a rhombus, $\overline{LM}$ ≅ _____.

(5) Step 5: Using the _____ Method,
△*LMX* ≅ △*LOY*.

(6) Conclusion: Since △*LMX* ≅ △*LOY*, $\overline{MX}$ ≅ _____.

3 State whether each of the following statements are true or false.
Write "T" for true and write "F" for false.

8 points each

(1) A square is always a rectangle. 〈Ans.〉 _____

(2) A rectangle is always a square. 〈Ans.〉 _____

(3) A rhombus is always a parallelogram. 〈Ans.〉 _____

(4) A rhombus might be a rectangle. 〈Ans.〉 _____

Name _____

Date _____ / ____ / ____   Score _____ /100

Remember It

Give these problems a try.

In each of the following problems, write the appropriate number in the box, so that each pair of ratios is equal.

1. $3:5 = 12:\boxed{}$

2. $\dfrac{2}{\boxed{}} = \dfrac{12}{18}$

Need a little help? Check out Review It before moving on.

⟨Ans.⟩ 1. 20   2. 3

Review It

The proportion of A to B is represented as $3:2$.
This is also called the **ratio** of A to B, and it is shown by the expression $A:B = 3:2$.

A [____|____|____] B [____|____]

The **value of a ratio** is the first term divided by the second term.

C [__|__]   D [_____] $C:D = 2:5 \rightarrow 2 \div 5 = \dfrac{2}{5}$

When both numbers in a ratio can be multiplied or divided by the same number those ratios are called **equivalent ratios**. The property of equivalent ratios states that the product of the outer terms is equal to the product of the inner terms.

$2:3 = 4:6$ (12, 12) $12:9 = 4:3$ (36, 36)

Ex. Find an equivalent ratio to $3:5$. $\rightarrow 3:5 = 4\times(3:5) = 12:20$, so $3:5 = 12:20$.

Ex. Find an equivalent ratio to $\dfrac{12}{18}$. $\rightarrow \dfrac{12}{18} = \dfrac{12}{18} \div \dfrac{6}{6} = \dfrac{2}{3}$, so $\dfrac{12}{18} = \dfrac{2}{3}$.

Practice It

1 **In each of the following problems, write the appropriate number in the box, so that each pair of ratios is equal.**

10 points each

(1) $\boxed{}:48 = 9:6$

(2) $\dfrac{\boxed{}}{4} = \dfrac{9}{6}$

(3) $\dfrac{20}{12} = \dfrac{\boxed{}}{3}$

pp. 1–65
Algebra

pp. 67–151
Geometry

pp. 153–183
Probability & Statistics

pp. 185–197
Review

2 Use △**ABC**, where $\overline{BO}$ = 2 in. and $\overline{OC}$ = 6 in., to answer the following questions.

10 points each

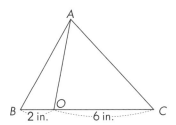

(1) What is the ratio of the measurement of $\overline{BO}$ to the measurement of $\overline{OC}$?

Since the ratio of $\overline{BO}$ to $\overline{OC}$ is 2 : 6, the ratio can be reduced to _____.

(2) What is the ratio of the measurement of $\overline{BO}$ to the measurement of $\overline{BC}$?

Since the measurement of $\overline{BO}$ is 2 in. and the measurement of $\overline{BC}$ is 8 in., the ratio is _____, which can be reduced to _____.

(3) What is the ratio of the area of △ABO to the area of △ABC?

The formula of the area of a triangle is _____, where the height is the same for both triangles, the ratio of the areas of the triangles is _____.

3 Given the figure, where line ℓ is parallel to line *m*, $\overline{BC}$ = 8 cm, and $\overline{EF}$ = 10 cm. Use this information to answer each of the following questions.

10 points each

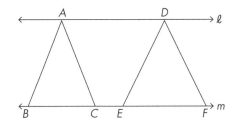

(1) What is the ratio of $\overline{BC}$ to $\overline{EF}$?

⟨Ans.⟩ _____

(2) If $\overline{BC}$ is the base of △ABC and $\overline{EF}$ is the base of △DEF, what is the ratio of the height of △ABC to the height of △DEF?

⟨Ans.⟩ _____

(3) What is the ratio of the area of △ABC to the area of △DEF?

⟨Ans.⟩ _____

4 Given parallelogram **EFGH**, where **O** is the midpoint of $\overline{FG}$. Find the ratio of the area of △**EOH** to the area of parallelogram **EFGH**.

10 points

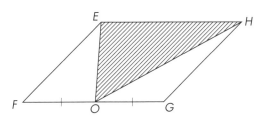

⟨Ans.⟩ _____

Quiz

Geometry 33

Geometry Quiz 4

Name

Date   /   /

Score   / 100

1 In the figure below, find the measurement of the missing angles.

10 points

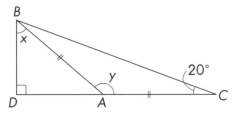

⟨**Ans.**⟩ $m\angle x =$ _____ , $m\angle y =$ _____

2 In the figure below, find the measurement of the missing angles.   10 points each

$\angle BAD = \angle DAC$, $m\angle BAC = 50°$

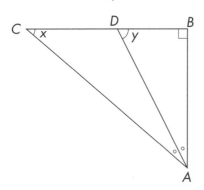

(1) What is the measurement of $\angle x$?

(a) 25°   (b) 40°   (c) 50°   (d) 65°

(2) What is the measurement of $\angle y$?

(a) 25°   (b) 40°   (c) 50°   (d) 65°

3 Given △ABC, where $\overline{AB} \cong \overline{AC}$ and $\overline{FB}$ and $\overline{DC}$ are angle bisectors. Prove that △EBC is an isosceles triangle by completing each of the following steps.

5 points each

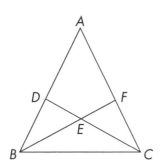

(1) Step 1: Since $\overline{FB}$ is an angle bisector, $\angle FBC = \frac{1}{2} \times$ _____.

(2) Step 2: Since $\overline{DC}$ is an angle bisector, $\angle DCB = \frac{1}{2} \times$ _____.

(3) Step 3: Since $\overline{AB} \cong \overline{AC}$, $\triangle ABC$ is a(n) _____ triangle.

(4) Step 4: Since $\triangle ABC$ is an isosceles triangle, therefore $\angle ABC \cong$ _____.

(5) Step 5: Since $\angle ABC \cong \angle ACB$ and $\angle FBC = \frac{1}{2} \times \angle ABC$ and $\angle DCB = \frac{1}{2} \times \angle ACB$, therefore

$\angle FBC \cong$ _____.

(6) Conclusion: Since $\angle FBC \cong \angle DCB$, therefore _____.

4 **In each of the following problems, write the shape of the parallelogram that best fits the description.**   5 points each

(1) A parallelogram with four congruent sides: _____.

(2) A parallelogram with four congruent angles: _____.

(3) A parallelogram with four congruent sides and four congruent angles: _____.

5 **Given the parallelogram *ABCD* is a rhombus. Prove that $\overline{BD}$ bisects both $\angle ABC$ and $\angle CDA$ by completing each of the following steps.**   5 points each

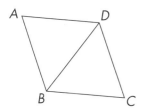

(1) Step 1: Since parallelogram $ABCD$ is a rhombus, therefore $\overline{AD} \cong \overline{DC} \cong$ _____.

(2) Step 2: Since parallelogram $ABCD$ is a parallelogram, therefore $\angle DAB \cong$ _____.

(3) Step 3: Using the _____ Method, therefore $\triangle ABD \cong$ _____.

(4) Step 4: Since $\triangle ABD \cong \triangle CBD$, therefore $\angle ABD \cong$ _____ and $\angle ADB \cong$ _____.

(5) Conclusion: Since $\angle ABD \cong \angle CBD$ and $\angle ADB \cong \angle CDB$, therefore _____

_____.

57

Transformations 1
Translation and Reflection

Geometry 34

Name

Date / /

Score / 100

Remember It

Give these problems a try.

1. Quadrilateral *ABCD* is provided on the grid. On the grid, draw another quadrilateral, *EFGH*, which is a translation of *ABCD* 8 units to the right and 2 units down.

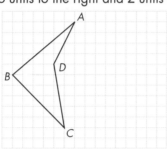

2. Line *AB* is provided on the grid. On the grid, draw another line, *CD*, which is a reflection across line ℓ.

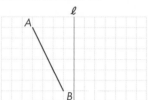

Need a little help? Check out Review It before moving on.

⟨**Ans.**⟩ 1. and 2. See answers in Review It.

Review It

Recall that a **translation** is a type of transformation where a figure is moved in certain directions without changing the shape or size.

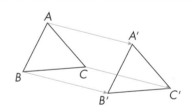

Ex. On the grid, draw quadrilateral *EFGH*, which is a translation of *ABCD* 8 units to the right and 2 units down. →

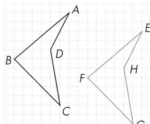

A **reflection** is a type of transformation where a figure is flipped over a **line of symmetry**. The figures before and after the reflection are congruent.

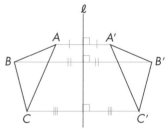

The folding line (ℓ) is the line of symmetry.

Ex. Line *AB* is provided on the grid. On the grid, draw another line, *CD*, which is a reflection across line ℓ. → Line *CD* is formed by flipping line *AB* over line ℓ.

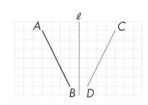

ⓒ *Kumon Publishing Co., Ltd.*

Practice It

1 **Quadrilateral *ABCD* is provided on the grid. Use the figure to answer each of the following questions.** 10 points each

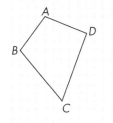

(1) Draw another quadrilateral, *EFGH*, which is a translation of quadrilateral *ABCD* 10 units to the right and 5 units down.

(2) Which side corresponds to $\overline{AD}$? 〈Ans.〉 _____

(3) Which angle corresponds to ∠*C*? 〈Ans.〉 _____

2 **Line *CD* is provided on the grid. On the grid, draw another line *EF*, which is a reflection over line ℓ.** 10 points

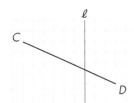

3 **Reflect each of the following shapes over the provided line of symmetry.** 12 points each

(1)

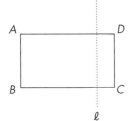

(2)

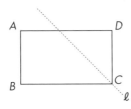

(3)

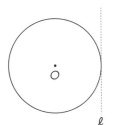

(4)

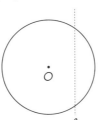

(5)

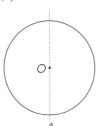

58 Transformations 2
Rotation, Point Symmetry, and Dilation

Name

Date   /   /   Score   / 100

Remember It

Give these problems a try.

1. Given △ABC. △ABC is rotated 45° counterclockwise around point O, the center of rotation. Draw the new triangle.

2. Given rectangle DEFG. It is rotated symmetrically around point P, the point of symmetry. Draw the new rectangle.

3. Given △HIJ on the grid. Each side of the triangle is then scaled up three times its original size. Draw the new triangle. (One side has already been drawn for you.)

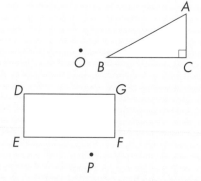

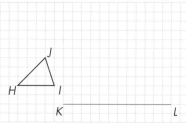

Need a little help? Check out Review It before moving on.

⟨Ans.⟩ 1.–3. See answer in Review It.

Review It

A **rotation** is a transformation that rotates a figure around a fixed point.

Ex. A new triangle is formed by rotating △ABC 45° counterclockwise around point O.

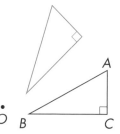

Recall that for **point symmetry**, a figure is rotated 180° around a fixed point.

Ex. The new rectangle is rotated 180° around point P.

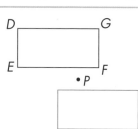

A **dilation** is a transformation where a figure changes size but keeps the same shape. In a dilation, the corresponding angles do not change. The corresponding sides change, but the ratios of the corresponding sides are all congruent.

Ex.

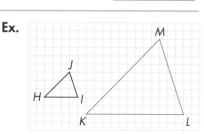

pp. 1–65
Algebra

pp. 67–151
Geometry

pp. 153–183
Probability & Statistics

pp. 185–197
Review

Practice It

1 Given quadrilateral *JKLM*. Use the figure to complete each of the following questions.

14 points each

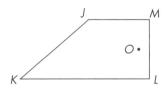

(1)   Quadrilateral *JKLM* is rotated 90° clockwise around point O. Draw the new quadrilateral.

(2)   Quadrilateral JKLM is rotated symmetrically around point O. Draw the new quadrilateral.

2 Categorize each of the following transformations. Write "T" for transformation, "Re" for reflection, "Ro" for rotation, and "D" for dilation.

12 points each

(1)

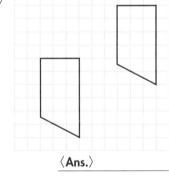

〈Ans.〉 _____

(2)

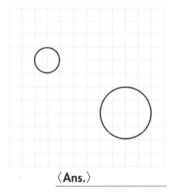

〈Ans.〉 _____

(3)

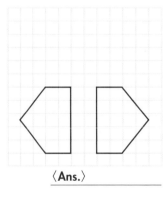

〈Ans.〉 _____

(4)

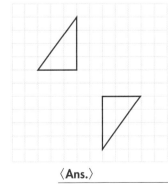

〈Ans.〉 _____

(5)

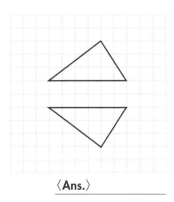

〈Ans.〉 _____

(6)

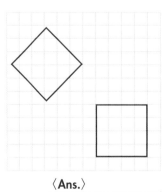

〈Ans.〉 _____

Name

Date   /   /   Score   / 100

Remember It

Give these problems a try.

△ABC ~ △DEF. Use this information to answer each of the following questions.

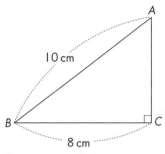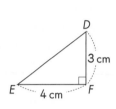

1. Find the scale factor of △ABC and △DEF.
2. Find the length of $\overline{DE}$.
3. Find the length of $\overline{AC}$.

Need a little help? Check out Review It before moving on.

⟨Ans.⟩ 1. 2 : 1   2. 5 cm   3. 6 cm

Review It

Figures with the same shape but different sizes are called **similar** figures. An enlarged or reduced figure is said to be similar to the original figure.

① In similar figures, ratios of corresponding sides are all proportional.
② In similar figures, corresponding angles are all congruent.
③ Similar figures are shown by using the symbol " ~ ".

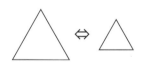

Ratios of corresponding sides of similar figures are congruent respectively. The ratio of corresponding sides is called the **scale factor**.

Ex. Find the scale factor of △ABC and △DEF, above. → Since △ABC and △DEF are similar to each other, the ratios of all corresponding sides are all proportional. The ratio of $\overline{BC}$ to $\overline{EF}$ is 8 : 4, which can be reduced to 2 : 1. So, the scale factor is 2 : 1.

Ex. Find the length of $\overline{DE}$. → Since the scale factor is 2 : 1, $\overline{DE}$ is half $\overline{AB}$. So, $\overline{DE}$ = 5 cm.

Ex. Find the length of $\overline{AC}$. → Since the scale factor is 2 : 1, $\overline{AC}$ is double $\overline{DF}$. So, $\overline{AC}$ = 6 cm.

ⓒ Kumon Publishing Co., Ltd.

Practice It

1 △OAB ~ △OA'B', as shown in the figure. Use the figure to answer each of the following questions.

8 points each

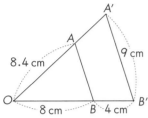

(1) Find the scale factor of △OAB and △OA'B'.

⟨Ans.⟩ _____ : _____

(2) Find the measurement of $\overline{AA'}$.

⟨Ans.⟩ _____

(3) Find the measurement of $\overline{OA'}$.

⟨Ans.⟩ _____

(4) Find the measurement of $\overline{AB}$.

⟨Ans.⟩ _____

2 Quadrilateral ABCD ~ EFGH, as shown in the figure, where the scale factor is 3 : 2. Use the figure to answer each of the following questions.

8 points each

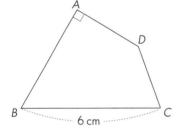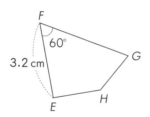

(1) Find m∠B.

⟨Ans.⟩ _____

(2) Find m∠E.

⟨Ans.⟩ _____

(3) Find $\overline{FG}$.

⟨Ans.⟩ _____

(4) Find $\overline{AB}$.

⟨Ans.⟩ _____

3 Given that △MNO ~ △PQR. State the missing conditions to prove similarity.

12 points each

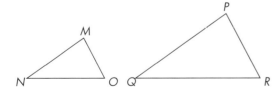

There are three ways to show that two triangles are similar:
① Show that the ratios of the measurements of all corresponding sides are congruent.
② Show that the ratio of the measurements of two corresponding sides are congruent and the corresponding angle between those two sides is congruent.
③ Show two sets of corresponding angles are congruent.

(1) $\overline{MN}:\overline{PQ} = \overline{NO}:\overline{QR} =$ _____

(2) $\overline{MN}:\overline{PQ} = \overline{NO}:\overline{QR}$ and ∠MNO ≅ _____

(3) ∠NOM ≅ ∠QRP and _____ ≅ _____

    or

 ∠NOM ≅ ∠QRP and _____ ≅ _____

Similar Triangles 2

Name

_____

Date _____ / _____ / _____   Score _____ / 100

Remember It

Give these problems a try.

Given △ABC, where ∠AED ≅ ∠ABC = 50°. Use this information to answer each of the following questions.

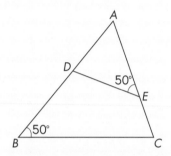

1. Which triangle is similar to △AED?
2. Which side corresponds to $\overline{DA}$?
3. Which angle corresponds to ∠ACB?

Need a little help? Check out Review It before moving on.

⟨Ans.⟩ 1. △ABC   2. $\overline{CA}$ 3. ∠ADE

Review It

Conditions for Similar Triangles

Similar triangles have at least one of the following conditions;

① The ratio of lengths of all corresponding sides are congruent.

② The ratio of lengths of two corresponding sides and the included angle are congruent respectively.

③ Two sets of corresponding angles are congruent respectively.

Ex. Which triangle is similar to △AED? → Since ∠AED ≅ ∠ABC = 50° and both triangles share ∠A, this means that △AED is similar to △ABC, by ③ showing that two sets of corresponding angles are congruent.

Ex. Which side corresponds to $\overline{DA}$? → △AED ∼ △ABC, so $\overline{DA}$ corresponds to $\overline{CA}$ since those points are in the same positions in the similarity expression.

Ex. Which angle corresponds to ∠ACB? → Since △AED ∼ △ABC, therefore ∠ACB corresponds to ∠ADE.

 ⓒ *Kumon Publishing Co., Ltd.*

pp. 1–65
Algebra

pp. 67–151
Geometry

pp. 153–183
Probability & Statistics

pp. 185–197
Review

Practice It

1 Find the measurement of side x in each of the following problems.

25 points each

(1) Given △ABC, where △ABC ~ △DBE and ∠ACB ≅ ∠BED = 90°.

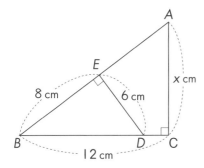

⟨Ans.⟩ _____

(2) Given △ABC, where △ABC ~ △DAC and ∠ABC ≅ ∠DAC.

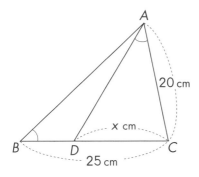

⟨Ans.⟩ _____

2 Given △ABC. Show that △ABC ~ △AED by completing each of the following steps.

25 points each

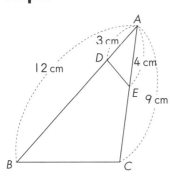

(1) Step 1: Since the scale factor of $\overline{AE} : \overline{AB} = \overline{AD} : \overline{AC} =$ _____ : _____ , this means that ratio of the

measurements of two corresponding sides are congruent.

(2) Step 2: Since both triangles share ∠A, △ ☐ ~ △ ☐ , since the corresponding angle

between the two sides is congruent.

Remember It

Give these problems a try.

Find the missing value, x, in each of the squares and the triangle.
Use a radical where applicable.

1.

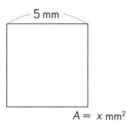

5 mm

$A = x$ mm^2

2.

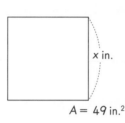

x in.

$A = 49$ in.^{2}

3.

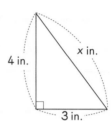

x in.

4 in.

3 in.

Need a little help? Check out Review It before moving on.

⟨**Ans.**⟩ 1. 25 mm^2 2. 7 in.   3. 5 in.

Review It

Recall that when a number is multiplied by itself, the result is called a **square number**. The result of squaring a whole number is called a **perfect square**. For example: $4 \times 4 = 16$, so 16 is a perfect square. The area of a square can be found by squaring the measurement of 1 side.

> **Ex.** Find the area of a square given the measure of one side is 5 mm. → $A = 5^2 = 25$ mm^2

The number b that satisfies $a = b^2$ is called a **square root** of a. For example, a square root of 25 is 5, because $5^2 = 25$. The square root of a positive number a is shown as $\sqrt{a}$. The measurement of one side of the square can be found by taking the square root of the area.

> **Ex.** Find the length of one side, x, of a square with an area of 49 in.^{2} → $x = \sqrt{49} = 7$ in.^{2}

The Pythagorean Theorem

In a right triangle, given that hypotenuse is c and the other two sides are a and b, the relationship $a^2 + b^2 = c^2$ is true.

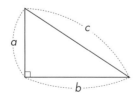

c

a

b

Ex. Find the length of the hypotenuse of a right triangle with legs measuring 4 inches and 3 inches.

$$a^2 + b^2 = c^2 \rightarrow 3^2 + 4^2 = x^2$$
$$9 + 16 = 25 = x^2$$
$$x = 5 \text{ in.}$$

pp. 1–65
Algebra

pp. 67–151
Geometry

pp. 153–183
Probability & Statistics

pp. 185–197
Review

Practice It

1 Find the missing value in each of the squares below.   5 points each

(1)

1.2 cm

$A = x$ cm²

The area of a square can be found by squaring the measurement of one side, so $A =$ _____ cm².

(2)

x cm

$A = 12$ cm²

Some square roots of non-perfect squares can be reduced. The result is not a whole number. Use $\sqrt{}$ (radical sign) to show non-perfect squares.

The measurement of one side of the square can be found by taking the _____ of the area, so $x = \sqrt{12} = \sqrt{4 \times 3} = \sqrt{2^2} \times \sqrt{3}$

= _____ cm.

2 Find the measurement of the missing value in each triangle.
Use a radical where applicable.   8 points each

(1)
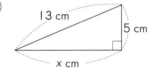
13 cm
5 cm
x cm

$a^2 + b^2 = c^2 \rightarrow 5^2 + x^2 = 13^2$
so, $x =$ _____ cm.

(2)
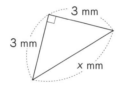
3 mm
3 mm
x mm

$a^2 + b^2 = c^2 \rightarrow 3^2 + 3^2 = x^2$
so, $x =$ _____ mm.

(3)
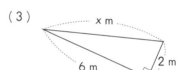
x m
6 m
2 m

$a^2 + b^2 = c^2 \rightarrow 6^2 + \boxed{} = \boxed{}$
so, $x =$ _____ m.

3 Find the missing value in each square.
Use a radical where applicable.   5 points each

(1)

3 in.

⟨Ans.⟩ $A =$ _____

(2)
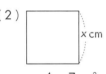
x cm
$A = 7$ cm²

⟨Ans.⟩ $x =$ _____

(3)

x m
$A = 50$ m²

⟨Ans.⟩ $x =$ _____

(4)

$\sqrt{5}$ m

⟨Ans.⟩ $A =$ _____

(5)

x mm
$A = 72$ mm²

⟨Ans.⟩ $x =$ _____

(6)

$2\sqrt{3}$ cm

⟨Ans.⟩ $A =$ _____

4 Find the measurement of the missing value in each triangle.
Use a radical where applicable.   6 points each

(1)
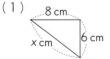
8 cm
x cm
6 cm

⟨Ans.⟩ $x =$ _____

(2)

8 m
17 m
x m

⟨Ans.⟩ $x =$ _____

(3)
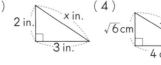
2 in.
x in.
3 in.

⟨Ans.⟩ $x =$ _____

(4)
$\sqrt{6}$ cm
x cm
4 cm

⟨Ans.⟩ $x =$ _____

(5)
2 m
1 m
x m

⟨Ans.⟩ $x =$ _____

(6)

1 in.
1 in.
x in.

⟨Ans.⟩ $x =$ _____

© Kumon Publishing Co., Ltd. 143

Remember It

Give these problems a try.

Given △ABC, where △ABC is a 30°–60°–90° triangle and $BC = 4$ m. Use this information to answer each of the following questions. Use a radical where applicable.

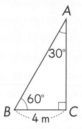

1. Find $\overline{AB}$.
2. Find $\overline{AC}$.

Need a little help? Check out Review It before moving on.

⟨Ans.⟩ 1. 8 m   2. 4√3 m

Review It

The ratio of the opposite sides in a **30°–60°–90° right triangle** is always **2 : 1 : √3**. (√3 is approximately 1.7.)

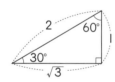

Ex. Given △ABC, where △ABC is a 30°–60°–90° triangle and $\overline{BC} = 4$ m, find $\overline{AB}$.

The ratio of the side opposite of 30° to the hypotenuse is 1 : 2.

$1 : 2 = 4 : 8$ So, $\overline{AB} = 8$ cm.

Ex. Find $\overline{AC}$ in △ABC.

The ratio of the side opposite of 30° to the side opposite of 60° is 1 : √3.

$1 : \sqrt{3} = 4 : 4\sqrt{3}$ So, $\overline{AC} = 4\sqrt{3}$ cm.

pp. 1–65
Algebra

pp. 67–151
Geometry

pp. 153–183
Probability & Statistics

pp. 185–197
Review

Practice It

1 Given △*DEF*, where *m∠E* = 90°, *m∠D* = 60°, and the hypotenuse is 5 in.
Use this information to answer the following questions.

10 points each

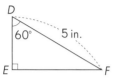

(1) Find $\overline{DE}$.

The ratio of the hypotenuse to the side opposite 30° is ____:____.

Since $\overline{DF}$ = 5 in., $\overline{DE}$ = _____ in.

(2) Find $\overline{EF}$.

The ratio of the hypotenuse to the side opposite 60° is ____:____.

Since $\overline{DF}$ = 5 in., $\overline{EF}$ = _____ in.

> When working radicals,
> it is often easier to write
> values in terms of fractions,
> instead of decimals.

2 Given △*ABC*, where △*ABC* is a 30°–60°–90° right triangle and $\overline{BC}$ = 3 cm.
Use this information to answer the following questions.

10 points each

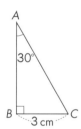

(1) Find $\overline{AB}$.

(2) Find $\overline{AC}$.

⟨Ans.⟩ _____

⟨Ans.⟩ _____

3 Given △*FGH*, where △*FGH* is a 30°–60°–90° right triangle and $\overline{FH}$ = 8√3 in.
Use this information to answer the following questions.

15 points each

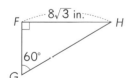

(1) Find $\overline{GH}$.

(2) Find $\overline{FG}$.

⟨**Ans.**⟩ _____

⟨**Ans.**⟩ _____

4 Given △*MNO*, where △*MNO* is a 30°–60°–90° right triangle and $\overline{NO}$ = 7 mm.
Use this information to answer the following questions.

15 points each

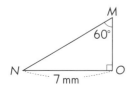

(1) Find $\overline{MO}$.

(2) Find $\overline{MN}$.

Remember to rationalize the
denominator in your answer.

⟨**Ans.**⟩ _____

⟨**Ans.**⟩ _____

63

Special Right Triangles 2
45°–45°–90° Triangles

Geometry 40

Name

Date ___/___/___

Score ___/100

Remember It

Give these problems a try.

Given △ABC, where △ABC is a 45°–45°–90° right triangle and $\overline{AC}$ = 3 in. Use this information to answer each of the following questions. Use a radical where applicable.

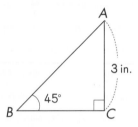

1. Find $\overline{BC}$.
2. Find $\overline{AB}$.

Need a little help? Check out Review It before moving on.

⟨Ans.⟩ 1. 3 in.   2. 3√2 in.

Review It

The ratio of the opposite sides in a **45°–45°–90° right triangle** is always: **1 : 1 : √2.** (√2 is approximately 1.4.)

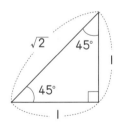

Ex. Given 45°–45°–90° right triangle △ABC, and $\overline{AC}$ = 3 in., find $\overline{BC}$.

The ratio of one leg to the other leg is 1 : 1. The legs of a 45°–45°–90° right triangle are always congruent.
$\overline{AC}$ = 3 in., so $\overline{BC}$ = 3 in.

Ex. Find $\overline{AB}$ in △ABC. → The ratio of either leg to the hypotenuse is 1 : √2 .
$\overline{AC}$ = 3 in., so $\overline{AB}$ = 3√2 in.

Practice It

1 Given △*DEF*, where △*DEF* is a 45°–45°–90° right triangle and $\overline{EF} = \sqrt{6}$ cm.
Use this information to answer each of the following questions.   20 points each

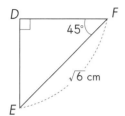

(1) Find $\overline{DE}$.

In a 45°–45°–90° right triangle, the ratio of a hypotenuse to either leg is ____:____.

$\overline{EF} = \sqrt{6}$ cm, so $\overline{DE} =$ _____ cm.

(2) Find $\overline{DF}$.

$\overline{EF} = \sqrt{6}$ cm, so $\overline{DF} =$ _____ cm.

2 Find the length of the two unknown sides from each of the following
45°–45°–90° right triangles.   20 points each

(1)

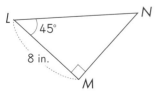

⟨**Ans.**⟩ $\overline{DE} =$ _____ , $\overline{EF} =$ _____

(2)

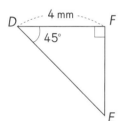

⟨**Ans.**⟩ $\overline{GH} =$ _____ , $\overline{HI} =$ _____

(3)

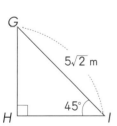

⟨**Ans.**⟩ $\overline{MN} =$ _____ , $\overline{LN} =$ _____

Remember It

Give these problems a try.

Given △ABC, where △ABC is an equilateral triangle with a side of 4 and $\overline{AO}$ bisects ∠A. Use this information to answer each of the following questions. Use a radical where applicable.

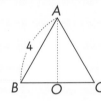

1. Find $\overline{BO}$.
2. Find $m\angle BAO$.
3. What type of special right triangle is △ABO?
4. Find $\overline{AO}$.

Need a little help? Check out Review It before moving on.

⟨Ans.⟩ 1. 2   2. 30°   3. 30°–60°–90° right triangle   4. 2√3

Review It

Recall that the angles in an equilateral triangle are all congruent and each measure 60°.

Ex. Since △ABC is an equilateral triangle, ∠ABC ≅ ∠BCA ≅ ∠CAB = 60° and all sides equal 4 units.

In an equilateral triangle, the bisector of a vertex angle bisects the base perpendicularly.

Ex. Find $\overline{BO}$, $\overline{AO}$, and $m\angle BAO$.

$\overline{AO}$ bisects ∠A, so $m\angle BAO = 30°$.
$\overline{AO}$ is a perpendicular bisector of $\overline{BC}$, so $\overline{BO} = 2$.
$m\angle ABO = 60°$ and $\angle BAO = 30°$, so △ABO is a 30°–60°–90° right triangle.
The ratio of the side opposite of 60° to the hypotenuse is $2 : \sqrt{3}$. So, $\overline{AO} = 2\sqrt{3}$.

Ex. Given the figure, where point P is at (2, 3) and point Q is at (7, 6). Find the measurement of $\overline{PQ}$.

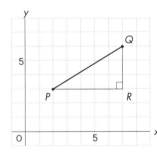

$\overline{PQ}$ is the hypotenuse of △PQR.
$\overline{PR} = 5$ and $\overline{QR} = 3$ → $5^2 + 3^2 = (\overline{PQ})^2$ So, $\overline{PQ} = \sqrt{34}$.

Practice It

1 Triangle **ABC** is an equilateral triangle with a side of 8 cm. The midpoint of $\overline{BC}$ is **M** and $\overline{AH} \cong \overline{BH} \cong \overline{CH}$. Use this information to answer each of the following questions.
(1) (2)15 points each, (3)20 points

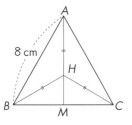

(1) Fill in the box:

The area of △HBC is ☐ the area of △ABC.

(2) Find the area of △HBC.
⟨Ans.⟩ _____

(3) Find $\overline{HM}$.
⟨Ans.⟩ _____

2 **Find the distance between each of the following pairs of points.**
(1) (2)15 points each, (3)20 points

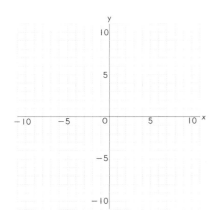

(1) (2, 3) and (5, 9)
⟨Ans.⟩ _____

(2) (−4, −1) and (2, −6)
⟨Ans.⟩ _____

(3) (x_1, y_1) and (x_2, y_2)
⟨Ans.⟩ _____

1 Given the triangle. Reflect the triangle over the line of symmetry.   **10 points**

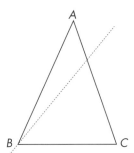

2 Given △ABC. The triangle is rotated symmetrically around point P. Draw the new triangle.   **10 points**

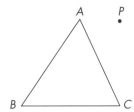

3 In the figure below, △OAB ∼ △OA′B′ . Use the information to answer each of the following questions.   **10 points each**

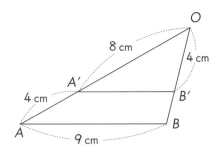

(1) Find the scale factor of △OAB and △OA′B′.

⟨Ans.⟩ _____

(2) Find the length of $\overline{BB'}$.

⟨Ans.⟩ _____

pp. 1–65
Algebra

pp. 67–151
Geometry

pp. 153–183
Probability & Statistics

pp. 185–197
Review

4 In each of the given figures, find the value of the missing side.
Use a radical where applicable.

20 points each

(1)

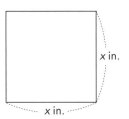

$A = 12$ in.^{2}

⟨**Ans.**⟩ $x =$ _____ in.

(2)

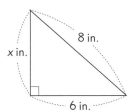

⟨**Ans.**⟩ $x =$ _____ in.

5 In each of the following triangles, find the measurement of the missing side.

10 points each

(1)

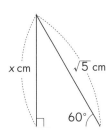

(a) $\dfrac{\sqrt{5}}{3}$ cm (b) $\dfrac{\sqrt{5}}{2}$ cm (c) $\dfrac{\sqrt{15}}{3}$ cm (d) $\dfrac{\sqrt{15}}{2}$ cm (e) 15 cm

(2)

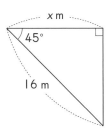

(a) 8 m (b) $8\sqrt{2}$ m (c) 16 m (d) $16\sqrt{2}$ m (e) 32 m

Memo

Kumon Math Workbooks

Grades **7** & **8**

Are You Ready for High School Math?

Probability & Statistics

Table of Contents

KUMON

Name

Date   /   /

Score   / 100

Remember It

Give these problems a try.

Determine the probability of the following.
1. Rolling a 6-sided number cube once and landing on an even number.
2. Selecting an ace from a deck of cards.
3. Flipping a dime once and landing on tails.

Need a little help? Check out Review It before moving on.

$\langle$Ans.$\rangle$ 1. $\frac{3}{6} = \frac{1}{2}$ 2. $\frac{4}{52} = \frac{1}{13}$ 3. $\frac{1}{2}$

Review It

You can use probability to predict if something is likely to happen. **Theoretical probability** is the ratio of the number of favorable outcomes to the total possible outcomes. The probability of any event happening is always between 0 and 1.

$$P(\text{event}) = \frac{\text{number of favorable outcomes}}{\text{total possible outcomes}}$$

Ex. Rolling a 6-sided number cube once and landing on an even number → $P(\text{even}) = \frac{3}{6}$
Since there are 3 even numbers on a number cube {2, 4, and 6} and a total of 6 possible outcomes {1, 2, 3, 4, 5, 6}.

The sum of probabilities of all possible outcomes will always be 1.

Ex. Flipping a dime once → $P(\text{heads}) = \frac{1}{2}$ $P(\text{tails}) = \frac{1}{2}$

$$P(\text{heads}) + P(\text{tails}) = \frac{1}{2} + \frac{1}{2} = 1$$

Practice It

1 **In a bag, there are 7 raffle tickets, each one with a unique number from 1 to 7 printed on it. Priya randomly picks 1 ticket from the bag.**
Determine the probability of the following events.   5 points each

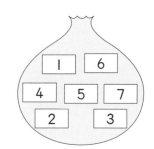

(1) What is the probability that Priya picks Ticket #4?

Since there is only 1 Ticket #4 out of 7 raffle tickets, $P(4) = \dfrac{\boxed{}}{7}$

© *Kumon Publishing Co., Ltd.*

(2) What is the probability that Priya picks Ticket #7?

⟨Ans.⟩ _____

(3) What is the probability that Priya picks a ticket that is an even number?

How many even numbers are there from 1 to 7?   ⟨Ans.⟩ _____

(4) What is the probability that Priya picks a ticket that is a multiple of 3?

⟨Ans.⟩ _____

(5) What is the probability that Priya picks a ticket that is a number from 1 to 5?

⟨Ans.⟩ _____

(6) What is the probability that Priya picks a ticket that is a number greater than 2?

⟨Ans.⟩ _____

2 **Priya flips a penny once. Determine the probability of the following events.**

15 points each

(1) What is the probability that the penny lands on heads?

$P(\text{heads}) = \dfrac{\square}{\square}$ Heads or tails are the only possible outcomes when flipping a penny.

(2) What is the probability that the penny lands on tails?

⟨Ans.⟩ _____

3 **Mr. Jones rolls a 6-sided number cube once. Determine the probability of the following events.**

10 points each

(1) $P(4) = \dfrac{\square}{\square}$

(3) $P(5) = \dfrac{\square}{\square}$

(2) $P(\text{odd}) = \dfrac{\square}{6} =$

(4) $P(1) = \dfrac{\square}{\square}$

© Kumon Publishing Co., Ltd. 155

Relative Frequency

Name

_____

Date ____/____/____   Score _____/100

Remember It

Give these problems a try.

A number cube has 6 sides, each labeled with a number from 1 to 6. Alexi rolls a number cube 20 times. His results are shown in the table.

Sides	1	2	3	4	5	6	Total
Frequency	4	3	4	3	2	4	20

What is the relative frequency that the number cube lands on each of the following numbers?

1. 6:   **2.** 4:   **3.** 2:

Need a little help? Check out Review It before moving on.

⟨Ans.⟩ 1. $\frac{4}{20}$ = 20%   2. $\frac{3}{20}$ = 15%   3. $\frac{3}{20}$ = 15%

Review It

As an experiment is repeated multiple times, the probability that an event occurs will usually approach a specific percentage. This percentage is known as the **relative frequency**.

$$\text{Relative frequency} = \frac{\text{frequency}\,(f)}{\text{total number of outcomes}\,(t)}$$

Ex. The relative frequency of landing on a 6: $\frac{f}{t} = \frac{4}{20} = 20\%$.

Relative frequency is usually given as a percentage.

Ex. Both 4 and 2 have the same relative frequency since they are both rolled 3 times each: $\frac{3}{20} = 15\%$

The more trials in an experiment, the closer the relative frequency will be to the theoretical probability.

Ex. Alexi rolls the number cube 10 more times. He wants to see how the relative frequency of rolling 5 changes. His results are shown in the table.

Number of Rolls	10	20	30	40
Frequency of 5	1	2	4	6
Relative Frequency	$\frac{1}{10} = 10\%$	$\frac{2}{20} = 10\%$	$\frac{4}{30} \approx 13.33\%$	$\frac{6}{40} = 15\%$

As the number of trials increases, the relative frequency approaches the theoretical probability $P(5) = \frac{1}{6} \approx 16.67\%$.

Relative frequency is also called **experimental probability**. Experimental probability can be used to make predictions.

pp. 1–65
Algebra

pp. 67–151
Geometry

pp. 153–183
Probability & Statistics

pp. 185–197
Review

Practice It

1 Ms. Smith says that if you flip a coin, there is a 50% chance that it lands on heads. Jack performs an experiment to test Ms. Smith's prediction. He flips a quarter 1,000 times and records the number of times that the quarter lands on heads. His results are shown in the following table.

Number of Flips	20	150	500	700	1,000
Frequency of Heads	6	57	264	343	500
Relative Frequency	$\frac{6}{20} = 30\%$	A	B	C	D

Calculate each of the missing values from the table.   8 points each

(1) A = $\dfrac{\boxed{}}{150}$ = _____ %

To find the percentage, divide the numerator by the denominator. Then multiply by 100.

(2) B = $\dfrac{\boxed{}}{\boxed{}}$ = _____ %

(4) D = $\dfrac{\boxed{}}{\boxed{}}$ = _____ %

(3) C = $\dfrac{\boxed{}}{\boxed{}}$ = _____ %

(5) Was Ms. Smith correct?

⟨Ans.⟩ _____

2 Tetrahedron-shaped dice have 4 sides. Each vertex on the tetrahedron has a number associated with it. The numbers 1, 2, 3, and 4 each represent one of the vertices. Priya rolls the tetrahedron 900 times and records the number of times that she rolls a 4. Her results are shown in the following table.

Rolls	16	75	250	600	800
Frequency of 4	2	12	80	162	201
Relative Frequency	A	B	C	D	E

Calculate each of the missing values from the table.   10 points each

(1) A = $\dfrac{\boxed{}}{\boxed{}}$ = _____ %

(4) D = $\dfrac{\boxed{}}{\boxed{}}$ = _____ %

(2) B = $\dfrac{\boxed{}}{\boxed{}}$ = _____ %

(5) E = $\dfrac{\boxed{}}{\boxed{}}$ = _____ %

(3) C = $\dfrac{\boxed{}}{\boxed{}}$ = _____ %

(6) Estimate the overall relative frequency based on your answers above.

Remember, the more trials, or rolls, there are, the more accurate the results will be.

⟨**Ans.**⟩ _____

Name _____

Date ___ / ___ / ___   Score _____ / 100

Remember It

Give these problems a try.

A box contains 4 cards, where each card has a colored animal printed on it: a red mouse, a green bird, a red dog, or a green cat. Eli randomly draws 1 card from the box.

1. What is the probability that a randomly selected card is blue?
2. What is the probability that a randomly selected card is either green or red?

Need a little help? Check out Review It before moving on.

⟨Ans.⟩ 1. $\frac{0}{4} = 0$ 2. $\frac{4}{4} = 1$

Review It

An event that has a probability of 0, or 0%, will not occur. This is called an *impossible event*. An outcome with a probability that is close to but not 0% is an *unlikely event*.

Ex. $P(\text{blue}) = 0$, since none of the possible outcomes is a blue card.

So, picking a blue card is impossible.

An event that has a probability of 1, or 100%, is guaranteed to occur. This is called a *certain event*. The closer a probability is to 1 or 100%, the more likely the event is to occur. An event with a probability that is close to 1 or 100% is a *likely event*.

Ex. $P(\text{green or red}) = \frac{4}{4} = 1$, since all of the outcomes are either green or red.

So, either a green or red card must be picked.

$P(\text{green or red})$ is called a **compound event**.

An outcome with a probability of 50%, or $\frac{1}{2}$, represents an event that is *neither likely nor unlikely*.

Ex. $P(\text{green}) = \frac{2}{4} = \frac{1}{2}$ so a green card is neither likely nor unlikely to be picked.

Practice It

1 **Determine the probability of each of the following events.**   10 points each

(1) What is the probability that Eli picks a card with a bird?

$P(\text{bird}) = \dfrac{\square}{\square} = \square\%$ ⟨**Ans.**⟩ _____

(2) What is the probability that Eli picks a green card?

⟨**Ans.**⟩ _____

© Kumon Publishing Co., Ltd.

pp. 1–65
Algebra

pp. 67–151
Geometry

pp. 153–183
Probability & Statistics

pp. 185–197
Review

(3) What is the probability that Eli picks a card with an animal?

⟨**Ans.**⟩ _____

(4) What is the probability that Eli picks a card with a lion?

⟨**Ans.**⟩ _____

(5) Which events above are unlikely to occur?

⟨**Ans.**⟩ _____

> An event that is close to but
> not 0% is an unlikely event.

2 **A standard deck of playing cards contains 52 cards, where each card has 3 identifying features: suit, color, and number (or face).**   5 points each

- The 4 suits are: spades (black), hearts (red), clubs (black), and diamonds (red).
- The number cards are 2, 3, 4, 5, 6, 7, 8, 9, and 10, because there is a number on the card.
- The face cards are jack, queen, and king, because there is a face on the card.
- The ace card does not have a number nor a face.
- Each suit includes the 9 number cards, 3 face cards, and 1 ace card.

Danny randomly draws 1 card from the pile.
Determine the probability of each of the following outcomes and state whether each event is certain, likely, unlikely, impossible, or none of the above.

(1) $P(\text{face card}) =$

> There are 3 face cards in each suit.

⟨**Ans.**⟩ _____

(2) $P(\text{red}) =$

⟨**Ans.**⟩ _____

(3) $P(\text{club or red}) =$

> Since the event uses the word "or," either a club OR a red card is a favorable outcome.

⟨**Ans.**⟩ _____

(4) $P(\text{heart or black}) =$

⟨**Ans.**⟩ _____

> Since the event uses the word "and," both must be true. Only cards that are both diamond AND red should be counted as a favorable outcome.

(5) $P(\text{diamond and red}) =$

⟨**Ans.**⟩ _____

(6) $P(\text{black and even}) =$

⟨**Ans.**⟩ _____

(7) $P(\text{black or even}) =$

⟨**Ans.**⟩ _____

(8) $P(\text{black or red}) =$

⟨**Ans.**⟩ _____

(9) $P(\text{diamond or heart}) =$

⟨**Ans.**⟩ _____

(10) $P(\text{diamond and even}) =$

⟨**Ans.**⟩ _____

Name

Date _____ / _____ / _____

Score _____ / 100

Remember It

Give these problems a try.

1. What is the number of possible outcomes if Juliana rolls two 6-sided number cubes at the same time?
2. What is the probability that Juliana rolls two 1s?

Need a little help? Check out Review It before moving on.

⟨**Ans.**⟩ 1. 36 possible outcomes   2. $P(1 \text{ and } 1) = \dfrac{1}{36}$

Review It

Experiments with more than one event are called **compound events**. The **sample space** of a probability experiment is the set of all possible outcomes.

Ex. The sample space when rolling two number cubes once is:

(1, 1) (1, 2) (1, 3) (1, 4) (1, 5) (1, 6) (2, 1) (2, 2) (2, 3) (2, 4) (2, 5) (2, 6)
(3, 1) (3, 2) (3, 3) (3, 4) (3, 5) (3, 6) (4, 1) (4, 2) (4, 3) (4, 4) (4, 5) (4, 6)
(5, 1) (5, 2) (5, 3) (5, 4) (5, 5) (5, 6) (6, 1) (6, 2) (6, 3) (6, 4) (6, 5) (6, 6)

Out of 36 possible outcomes, only one outcome is (1, 1), so $P(1 \text{ and } 1) = \dfrac{1}{36}$.

To find the probability of a compound event that uses the word AND, multiply the probabilities of each individual event.

Ex. $P(1 \text{ and } 1) \rightarrow P(1) \times P(1) = \dfrac{1}{6} \times \dfrac{1}{6} = \dfrac{1}{36}$

A sample space can be organized as a list, table, or a **tree diagram**. A tree diagram provides a visual display of the sample space.

Ex. The sample space for choosing between two pairs of pants and three shirts is:
There are 6 possible outcomes.

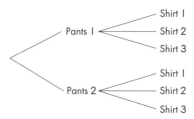

Practice It

1 Riley holds a bag that has 3 marbles: a blue marble, a green marble, and a purple marble. Riley randomly chooses one marble from the bag. The tree diagram below shows all the possible results.
Use the information to answer the following questions.   8 points each

> Notice that the tree diagram has branches, like the branches of a tree!

(1) Fill in the missing value from the diagram.

(2) $P(\text{blue}) = $ _____

(3) $P(\text{green}) = $ _____

(4) $P(\text{purple}) = $ _____

(5) $P(\underline{\text{NOT}}\ \text{purple}) = $ _____

> $P(\underline{\text{NOT}}\ \text{event}) = 1 - P(\text{event})$, or
> $P(\underline{\text{NOT}}\ \text{event}) = 100\% - P(\text{event})$

Marble Choice

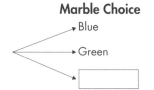

2 Angel flips a quarter twice. The tree diagram below shows all the possible outcomes, where H is heads and T is tails.
Use this information to answer the following questions.   15 points each

(1) Fill in each of the missing values from the diagram.

A: _____   B: _____

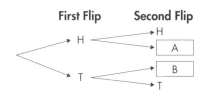

(2) When flipping the quarter once, the probability of landing on heads is:

$P(\text{H}) = \dfrac{\boxed{}}{\boxed{}} = \boxed{}\ \%$

> Count the number of H's in the diagram.
> The probability of landing on tails is:
> $P(\text{T}) = \dfrac{1}{2} = 50\ \%$

(3) When flipping the quarter twice, the probability of landing on heads both times is:

$P(\text{HH}) = \dfrac{\boxed{}}{\boxed{}} \times \dfrac{\boxed{}}{\boxed{}} = \dfrac{\boxed{}}{\boxed{}} = \boxed{}\ \%$

(4) When flipping the quarter twice, $P(\text{H and T})$, the probability of landing on heads once and tails once contains two possibilities: HT or TH.

$P(\text{HT}) = $

$P(\text{TH}) = $

Add these two probabilities to find $P(\text{H and T}) = $

Remember It

Give these problems a try.

Decide if the following represent a sample or a population.

1. Which is considered a population: everyone in the country or one person from each state?
2. Which is considered a sample: all the wolves in an area or 500 randomly chosen wolves?

Need a little help? Check out Review It before moving on.

⟨Ans.⟩ 1. Everyone in the country   2. 500 randomly chosen wolves

Review It

When researchers want to analyze a **population**, or specific group, they would obtain the most accurate results by collecting data from the whole population. A study, also called a **survey**, on an entire population is called a **census**.

Ex. The United States government conducts a special survey every 10 years. Every person living in the country must fill out the census.

However, it is often impractical to study an entire population, so researchers will instead study a smaller representation, or **sample**, of that population. A survey that is based on a sample of the population is called a **sample survey**.

Ex. Scientists tag a sample of wolves in the wilderness to collect information and make predictions about the entire population of wolves in that area.

Practice It

1 **For each scenario, write "P" if the entire population should be studied or "S" if it is better to study a sample of the population.**   10 points each

(1) The number of students in a particular school: _____

A population relates to the whole, or total.

(2) Favorite ice cream flavor: _____

(3) The average number of children in a family: _____

(4) The number of cars in a country: _____

(5) The number of dogs in a specific pet store: _____

2 There are 2,500 students in a high school. Leo randomly selects 100 students from the school to be interviewed.
Use this information to answer each of the following questions. *10 points each*

(1) What is the number of people in the entire population? ⟨**Ans.**⟩ _____

(2) How many people are in the sample survey? ⟨**Ans.**⟩ _____

3 Some fish in a river are orange and the rest of the fish are yellow. A scientist decides to catch 20 fish and analyze the results. There are 3,000 fish in the river. The scientist then releases the 20 fish and repeats this experiment 4 more times, where the results are shown below: *10 points each*

	Orange	Yellow
Experiment #1	8	12
Experiment #2	10	10
Experiment #3	7	13
Experiment #4	2	18
Experiment #5	9	11
Average	A	B

(1) Calculate each of the averages.

▶ Average number of orange fish: _____

▶ Average number of yellow fish: _____

(2) Using your data from the previous problem, estimate the percentage of orange fish and the percentage of yellow fish in the river.

▶ Estimated percentage of orange fish: $\frac{7.2}{20} = \boxed{}$ %

▶ Estimated percentage of yellow fish: _____

(3) Estimate the number of orange fish and the number of yellow fish in the river.

▶ Estimated number of orange fish: $\boxed{}$ % × 3,000 =

▶ Estimated number of yellow fish: _____

You can make a prediction for the population by multiplying the probability from the sample by the amount in the population.

Name _____

Date ____ / ____ / ____   Score _____ / 100

Remember It

Give these problems a try.

Ms. Rivera surveys several randomly selected middle-school students to find out their grade and how they arrive at school. Her results are listed below:

- 7th grade and car: 12 students
- 7th grade and bus: 36 students
- 8th grade and car: 22 students
- 8th grade and bus: 10 students

1. How many students did Ms. Rivera survey?
2. What is the probability that a student interviewed by Ms. Rivera is in the 7th grade and takes the bus to school?

Need a little help? Check out Review It before moving on.

⟨**Ans.**⟩ **1.** 80 students   **2.** $\frac{36}{80}$ = 45 %

Review It

When more than one variable is considered in a probability experiment, a **two-way table** can be used to organize the information.

Ex. The two variables in Ms. Rivera's survey are grade and transportation.

		Transportation	
		Car	**Bus**
Grade	**7th Grade**		
	8th Grade		

A column and row are usually added for totals so that the two-way table can be used to find various probabilities.

Ex. How many total students did Ms. Rivera interview?

	Car	Bus	Total
7th Grade	12	36	**48**
8th Grade	22	10	**32**
Total	**34**	**46**	**80**

The bottom right cell of the table shows the total number of students interviewed, 80 students.

Ex. What is the probability that a student interviewed by Ms. Rivera is in the 7th grade and takes the bus to school?

$\frac{36}{80}$ = 45%   45% of the students interviewed were both in 7th grade AND take the bus.

Ex. What is the probability that a 7th grade student takes the bus to school?

Look across the 7th grade row to find the total number of 7th graders: 48.

$\frac{36}{48}$ = 75%   75% of 7th graders take the bus.

 © Kumon Publishing Co., Ltd.

Practice It

1 **Use the two-way table from Ms. Rivera's survey to answer each of the following questions.** 16 points each

(1) What is the probability that a student interviewed by Ms. Rivera is an 8th grade student?

〈Ans.〉 _____

(2) What is the probability that a student takes the bus to school?

〈Ans.〉 _____

(3) What is the probability that a student does not take the bus to school?

〈Ans.〉 _____

(4) What is the probability that an 8th grade student arrives to school in a car?

〈Ans.〉 _____

2 **Jake and Olivia each rolled a 3-sided number cube. They recorded the sum of the numbers they roll in the table below:**

Olivia

		1	2	3
	1	2	3	4
Jake	2	3	4	5
	3	4	5	6

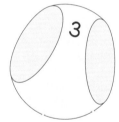

Use this information to answer each of the following questions. 12 points each

(1) How many total possible outcomes are there?

Since there are ☐ possible outcomes for Jake and there are ☐ possible outcomes for Olivia, there is a total of ☐ possible outcomes.

(2) What is the probability that the sum is 5?

Since there are ☐ possible outcomes where the sum is 5, the probability is: _____ .

(3) What is the probability that the sum is NOT 5?

〈Ans.〉 _____

Name

Date   /   /   Score   / 100

1 In a bag, there are 6 cards, where each card has a different colored shape printed on it. The 6 different designs are: a red circle, a green diamond, a blue square, a brown X, a green rectangle, and a blue triangle. Luis randomly chooses 1 card from the bag. Determine the probability of each of the following situations.   10 points each

(1)   What is the probability that Luis chooses a card with a blue shape printed on it?

⟨**Ans.**⟩ _____

(2)   What is the probability that Luis does <u>NOT</u> pick a card with a letter printed on it?

⟨**Ans.**⟩ _____

(3)   What is the probability that Luis picks a card with a 4-sided shape printed on it?

⟨**Ans.**⟩ _____

(4)   Is it likely or unlikely that Luis picks a card with a red shape printed on it?

⟨**Ans.**⟩ _____

2 In a box, there is a green marble, a blue marble, and a yellow marble. Susie randomly selects a marble from the box. She records the color, puts the marble back into the box, and then randomly selects a marble again and records the color. Determine the probability of each of the following situations.   10 points each

(1)   What is the probability that Susie picks the blue marble twice?

⟨**Ans.**⟩ _____

(2)   What is the probability that Susie picks 1 blue marble and 1 green marble?

⟨**Ans.**⟩ _____

3 There are 680 toys in a large container, where some toys are gray and the rest are purple. A worker randomly selects 12 toys and analyzes the results. The worker then places the toys back into the container and repeats the experiment 3 more times. The results are shown in the table below:

	Gray	Purple
Experiment #1	3	9
Experiment #2	7	5
Experiment #3	2	10
Experiment #4	6	6
Average	4.5	7.5

Estimate the number of gray-colored toys and the number of purple-colored toys in the container.

10 points

⟨Ans.⟩ Gray: _____ Purple: _____

4 Lee goes to a park and sees many pets in the park. She records the types of pets and what color they are in the table below:

	Dog	Cat
Brown	20	8
White	4	16

Use this information to answer each of the following questions.

10 points each

(1) How many pets did Lee see?

    (a) 20 pets   (b) 24 pets   (c) 28 pets   (d) 48 pets   (e) 96 pets

(2) What is the probability that Lee saw a white dog?

    (a) $\dfrac{4}{20}$ (b) $\dfrac{4}{24}$ (c) $\dfrac{4}{48}$ (d) $\dfrac{20}{48}$ (e) $\dfrac{20}{24}$ (f) $\dfrac{24}{48}$

(3) What is the probability that Lee saw a brown pet?

    (a) $\dfrac{8}{28}$ (b) $\dfrac{8}{48}$ (c) $\dfrac{20}{28}$ (d) $\dfrac{20}{24}$ (e) $\dfrac{28}{48}$

Frequency Distribution and Histograms

Name _____

Date ____ / ____ / ____   Score _____ / 100

Remember It

Give these problems a try.

Deon interviews 8 friends about the number of pets they own. His data is shown below:

    0   3   1   2
    1   4   4   0

Use the data to fill in each of the missing frequency values in the table below:

Number of Pets	Frequency
0	2
1	A :
2	B :
3	C :
4	D :
5	E :

Need a little help? Check out Review It before moving on.

(**Ans.**) A. 2 B. 1 C. 1 D. 2 E. 0

Review It

A **frequency table** can be used to organize and display how often certain data occur in an experiment.

Ex. Based on Deon's data, what is the frequency of 1 pet? → There are two 1s in Deon's data, so the frequency of 1 pet is 2.

Number of Pets	Frequency
1	2

An **interval** includes all the numbers between two given numbers. Data is often organized in intervals in frequency tables.

Ex. The interval 0–2 includes the numbers 0, 1, and 2. The frequency of 0–2 in Deon's data is 5.

Number of Pets	Frequency
0–2	5
3–5	3

A **histogram** is a type of bar graph that shows the frequency of values within certain intervals occurring within a data set.

Ex. The histogram to the right displays Deon's data visually.

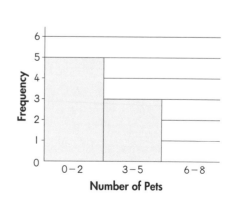

Practice It

1 **Ms. Lee interviews 20 people and asks them their height, in inches. The data is displayed below:**

```
69    57    55    72    60
65    62    67    69    71
54    56    61    63    72
61    76    69    77    65
```

Use the data to fill in each of the missing frequency values in the table below.

15 points each

Height (inches)	Frequency
51 – 55	2
56 – 60	A :
61 – 65	B :
66 – 70	C :
71 – 75	D :
76 – 80	E :

2 **Pilar is training to run in a race and keeps track of the time it takes her to run 1 mile, in minutes. Her data is displayed in the frequency table below:**

Time (minutes)	Frequency
8.1 – 8.5	2
8.6 – 9.0	3
9.1 – 9.5	1
9.6 – 10.0	1
10.1 – 10.5	2
10.6 – 11.0	1
11.1 – 11.5	2

Use the data to complete the histogram to display the frequency data. 25 points

(The first two intervals have been completed for you.)

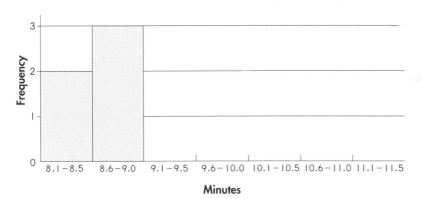

Since there are no values in between intervals, the bars in a histogram will usually touch.

Maximum, Minimum, and Range

Name _____

Date ___/___/___   Score ___/100

Remember It

Give these problems a try.

A middle school track coach records each of 10 team member's fastest mile runs. Their times are shown in this format : *minutes* : *seconds*

8:40	9:20	8:55	10:05	8:30
8:20	8:56	9:58	8:31	10:20

Use the data to answer the following questions.

1. What was the maximum time?
2. What was the minimum time?
3. What was the range of the data?

Need a little help? Check out Review It before moving on.

(**Ans.**) 1. 10:20   2. 8:20   3. 2:00

Review It

The greatest value of a data set is called the **maximum value**.
 Ex. What is the maximum value of the track coach's data?

The greatest value in the data is 10:20, so that is the maximum value.

The least value of a data set is called the **minimum value**.
 Ex. What is the minimum value of the track coach's data?

The least value in the data is 8:20, so that is the minimum value.

The **range** of values is the difference between the maximum value and the minimum value.
 Range   =   Maximum Value   −   Minimum Value

 Ex. What was the range of the data?

```
    10 minutes 20 seconds
  −  8 minutes 20 seconds
     2 minutes  0 seconds
```

So, the range is 2 minutes or 2:00.

pp. 1–65
Algebra

pp. 67–151
Geometry

pp. 153–183
Probability & Statistics

pp. 185–197
Review

 Practice It

1 **A meteorologist records the daily average temperature, in °F, of a city for 12 days in September. The data is shown below:**

(1)10 points, (2)–(4)15 points each

70	80	65	62	64	68
72	67	68	70	71	68

(1) Sort the values from greatest to least.

(The greatest value has been provided.)

80, ____, ____, ____, ____, ____, ____, ____, ____, ____, ____, ____

(2) The maximum temperature is: ☐ °F

The greatest value in a data set is the maximum. The least value is the minimum.

(3) The minimum temperature is: ☐ °F

(4) The range of temperatures is: 80°F − 62°F = ☐ °F

2 **Luca tracks how many cups of coffee are sold during each hour in his coffee shop. His data is displayed below:**

15 points each

40	52	60	68	54
50	62	68	70	50
40	32	20	8	10

(1) Find the maximum value.

⟨Ans.⟩ _____

(2) Find the minimum value.

⟨Ans.⟩ _____

(3) Find the range.

⟨Ans.⟩ _____

The range is the difference between the maximum and minimum values.

Remember It

Give these problems a try.

Sunil collects data about the monthly cost of various cell phone plans. His data is shown below:

$69	$40	$50	$33	$81	$20
$40	$78	$68	$40	$70	$71

Use the data to find the following values.

1. mean = _____   2. median = _____   3. mode = _____

Need a little help? Check out Review It before moving on.

⟨Ans.⟩ 1. $55   2. $59   3. $40

Review It

Measures of central tendency can tell us a lot about a typical member of a population. The average value of a data set is known as the **mean**. The mean can be found by adding all of the data values, then dividing by the number of data points.

Ex. Find the mean monthly cost of a cell phone plan based on Sunil's data.

$$\text{Mean} = \frac{\text{sum of all data}}{\text{number of data}}$$

$$= \frac{69 + 40 + 50 + 33 + 81 + 20 + 40 + 78 + 68 + 40 + 70 + 71}{12}$$

$$= \frac{660}{12}$$

$$= 55$$

The mean monthly cost of a cell phone plan is $55.

The middle value of a data set is known as the **median**. To find the median, order the data from least to greatest, then find the middle value. If there are two values in the middle, the median is the average of those two numbers.

Ex. Find the median monthly cost of a cell phone plan.

Order from least to greatest: 20, 33, 40, 40, 40, 50, 68, 69, 70, 71, 78, 81
50 and 68 are both middle values, so find the average.

$$\frac{50 + 68}{2} = \frac{118}{2} = 59$$

The median monthly cost of a cell phone plan is $59.

The value that occurs the most is known as the **mode**. There can be more than one mode in a data set.

Ex. Find the mode from Sunil's data.
The value that occurs most often is $40, so that is the mode.

Each of these values—the mean, median, or mode—can be used to describe a typical value from Sunil's data.

Practice It

1 **Mr. Cho records the scores that 15 students received on an assignment. The data is listed below:**

16 points each

6   3   3   8   9   10   8   2   4   6   8   5   8   3   10

(1) What was the average score?

⟨Ans.⟩ _____

(2) Order the values from least to greatest.

⟨Ans.⟩ _____

(3) Which score is in the middle after you order the scores from least to greatest?

⟨Ans.⟩ _____

(4) Which score occurs the most?

⟨Ans.⟩ _____

2 **Unique asks 25 friends how many pets they have at home. The data she collected is listed below:**

12 points each

1	0	5	2	3
1	0	0	1	2
1	2	4	2	1
0	3	3	1	1
6	1	0	2	3

(1) Find the mean.

⟨Ans.⟩ _____

(2) Find the median.

Remember to order the data before you look for the center number when finding the median.

⟨Ans.⟩ _____

(3) Find the mode.

⟨Ans.⟩ _____

Name

Date   /   /

Score   / 100

Remember It

Give these problems a try.

The numbers from 3 to 11 are given as a data set.

3   4   5   5   6   7   8   8   9   10   11

Find the following values based on the data set.

1. Quartile 1 : _____
2. Quartile 3 : _____
3. Interquartile Range: _____

Need a little help? Check out Review It before moving on.

⟨Ans.⟩ 1. 5   2. 9   3. 4

Review It

Recall that when ordering data, the median is the middle value of the data set. So, half of the data is below the median and the other half of the data is above the median.

The data set of values below the median is called the **lower half**. The median of the lower half is called the **lower quartile**, or **Q1**.

The data set of values above the median is called the **upper half**. The median of the upper half is called the **upper quartile**, or **Q3**.

Ex. Label the values in the number line that represent the lower half, upper half, median, Q1, and Q3.

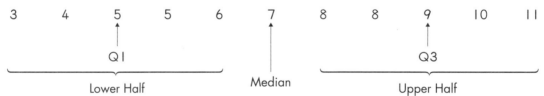

3   4   5   5   6   7   8   8   9   10   11

Q1   Median   Q3

Lower Half   Upper Half

The **interquartile range (IQR)** is the difference between Q3 and Q1.

IQR = Q3 − Q1

Ex. Find the interquartile range of the data.

IQR = 9 − 5 = 4

| pp. 1–65 | pp. 67–151 | pp. 153–183 | pp. 185–197 |
| Algebra | Geometry | **Probability & Statistics** | Review |

 Practice It

1 **Vincent goes to the beach every day and collects seashells. He records the number of seashells that he collects each day for 11 days. The data is shown below:**

10 points each

5 8 6 10 11 7 3 8 5 4 9

(1) Find the median.

Don't forget to first reorder the
values from smallest to largest.

⟨Ans.⟩ _____

(2) List the numbers that are below the median. Then list the median out of these numbers.

Half of the data is below the
median, or 5 numbers.

⟨Ans.⟩ _____

(3) List the numbers that are above the median. Then list the median out of all these numbers.

⟨Ans.⟩ _____

(4) Find the IQR of the number of seashells that Jack collects.

⟨Ans.⟩ _____

2 **Amani practices piano every day. She records how many minutes she practices each day for one week. The data is shown below:**

15 points each

25   50   45   40   35   45   30

(1) Find the median.

⟨Ans.⟩ _____

(2) Find the lower quartile, Q1.

⟨Ans.⟩ _____

(3) Find the upper quartile, Q3.

⟨Ans.⟩ _____

(4) Find the IQR.

⟨Ans.⟩ _____

© Kumon Publishing Co., Ltd.   175

Remember It

Give these problems a try.

Adina creates the following box-and-whisker plot.

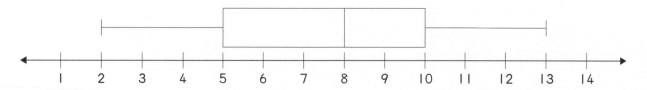

Use the box-and-whisker plot to find the following values:

1. Q1 : _____
2. Median: _____
3. Maximum: _____

Need a little help? Check out Review It before moving on.

⟨Ans.⟩ 1. 5   2. 8   3. 13

Review It

For a set of data, the minimum, Q1, median, Q3, and maximum can be displayed on a graph called a **box-and-whisker plot**:

Minimum   Q1   Median   Q3   Maximum

Ex. Find each of the following values based on Adina's plot.

Minimum: The line for the minimum is above 2. → 2

Q1: The line for Q1 is above 5. → 5

Median: The line for the median is above 8. → 8

Q3: The line for Q3 is above 10. → 10

Maximum: The line for the maximum is above 13. → 13

IQR: $10 - 5 = 5$

Practice It

1 **Ms. Brown records how many points her sports team scores in each game. The data is shown below:**

25 points each

4   5   9   3   4   10   11   13   7   9   3   2   5   6   8

(1) Find the minimum, Q1, median, Q3, and maximum.

Minimum: _____

Q1: _____

Median: _____

Q3: _____

Maximum: _____

(2) Create a box-and-whisker plot based on Ms. Brown's data.

Points Scored

2 **Dr. Lee records how many cats are brought into his animal hospital each day. The data is shown below:**

25 points each

5   2   8   10   4   13   9   6   4   3   7

(1) Create a histogram to represent Dr. Lee's data.

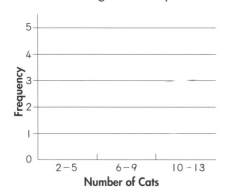

(2) Create a box-and-whisker plot to represent Dr. Lee's data.

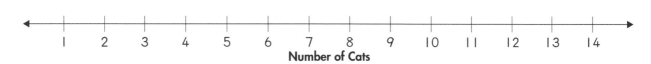

Number of Cats

Scatterplots

Name

Date   /   /   Score   / 100

Remember It

Give these problems a try.

Kimberly interviews several of her friends and asks them about their age and their height, in inches.

Age	Height (inches)	Age	Height (inches)
8	52	13	60
12	53	9	50
10	51	14	63
12	58	13	61

1. Use the data in the table to complete the scatterplot.

2. Based on this scatterplot, what is the relationship between age and height?

3. Do age and height have a positive correlation, negative correlation, or no correlation?

Need a little help? Check out Review It before moving on.

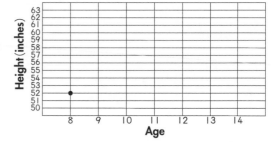

(Ans.) 1. See the completed scatterplot in Review It.   **2.** As age goes up, height goes up.   **3.** Positive correlation

Review It

Often we need to study the relationship between two separate categories of data such as: age and height, or weight of food and calories in food.

We can express each data item as a point on a graph. This type of graph is called a **scatterplot**.

When a pattern appears in a scatterplot, we say that the variables are **correlated** to one another. This means that they are related.

- In a **positive correlation**, when one variable increases, so does the other. The points rise from left to right.
- For a **negative correlation**, when the x-value increases, the y-value decreases. The data move downward.
- When there is no **correlation**, there is no apparent pattern in the scatterplot. The variables are likely unrelated.

Ex.

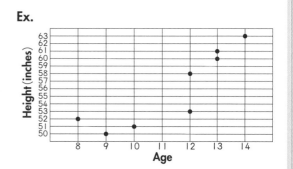

Positive Correlation   **Negative Correlation**   **No Correlation**

Practice It

1 **Bella sells several different types of cookies at her cookie shop. She keeps track of each customer that comes into her shop and records how many total cookies they purchase and how much they spent in total. Her records are shown below.**   25 points each

Cookies Bought	Total Spent (in dollars)	Cookies Bought	Total Spent (in dollars)
5	10	2	5
1	3	1	2
4	10	7	11
6	14	5	9
4	15	3	9

(1) Create a scatterplot based on Bella's data.

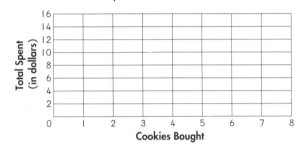

(2) Based on this scatterplot, what is the relationship between the number of cookies bought and the total spent?

⟨Ans.⟩ _____

(3) Do amount bought and total spent have a positive correlation, negative correlation, or no correlation?

⟨Ans.⟩ _____

2 **What variables might have a negative correlation with age?**   25 points

⟨Ans.⟩ _____

Name _____

Date ___/___/___   Score _____/100

Remember It

Give these problems a try.

Mr. Gomez wanted to find out the relationship between the time his students spent studying and the number of errors they had on the most recent biology test. He plotted his data in the scatterplot below:

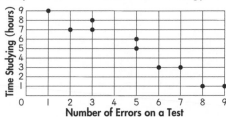

Use this information to answer the following questions.

1. What type of correlation does the data have?
2. In the scatterplot, draw the line of best fit for the data.

Need a little help? Check out Review It before moving on.

⟨Ans.⟩ **1.** Negative correlation   **2.** See the completed graph in Review It.

Review It

For data whose variables are correlated, we can use the scatterplot to identify a straight line that best expresses the relationship between the two categories of data. This line is known as the **Line of Best Fit**.

The line of best fit can be used to analyze the type of correlation between the data. For example, a line of best fit that increases from left to right shows that there is a positive correlation between the variables. When one variable increases, the other increases as well.

Ex.

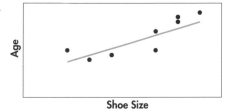

A line of best fit that decreases from left to right shows that there is a negative correlation between the variables. When one variable decreases, the other increases.

Ex.

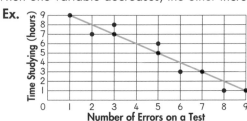

© Kumon Publishing Co., Ltd.

pp. 1–65
Algebra

pp. 67–151
Geometry

**pp. 153–183
Probability & Statistics**

pp. 185–197
Review

Practice It

1 **Identify which line is the most accurate Line of Best Fit for the scatterplot.**

25 points each

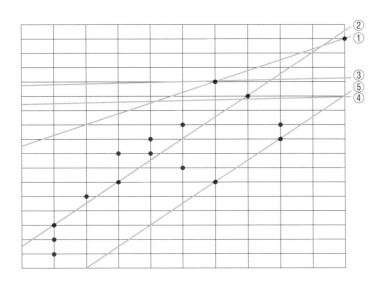

（1） What type of correlation does the data have?   〈Ans.〉 _____

（2） The line that represents the Line of Best Fit is: 〈Ans.〉 _____

2 **Identify which line is the most accurate Line of Best Fit for the scatterplot.**

25 points each

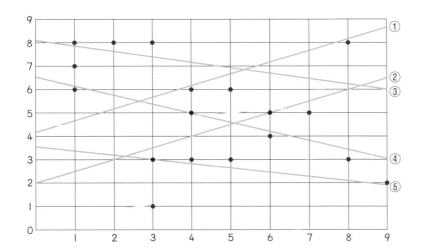

（1） What type of correlation does the data have?   〈Ans.〉 _____

（2） The line that represents the Line of Best Fit is: 〈Ans.〉 _____

Statistics Quiz

Name

_____

Date _____ / ___ / ___   Score _____ /100

1 Mr. Brown records how many points each student in his class received on an exam. His data is displayed in the frequency chart below: **25 points**

Points	Frequency
1 – 15	3
16 – 30	5
31 – 45	9
46 – 60	12
61 – 75	6

Use the data to draw a histogram that displays the frequency data.

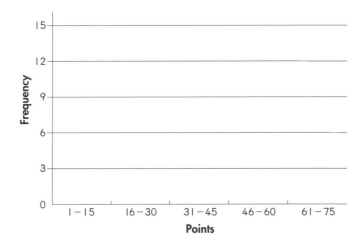

2 Coach Green records how many minutes it takes for her athletes to warm up each day. The data is listed below:

10 points each

8 6 10 9 5 15 18 20 16 12 15 9 15 8 11

(1) What is the mean of Coach Green's data?

  (a) 8   (b) 9.8   (c) 11   (d) 11.8   (e) 15   (f) 20

(2) What is the median of Coach Green's data?

  (a) 8   (b) 9.8   (c) 11   (d) 11.8   (e) 15   (f) 20

(3) What is the mode of Coach Green's data?

  (a) 8   (b) 9.8   (c) 11   (d) 11.8   (e) 15   (f) 20

 © Kumon Publishing Co., Ltd.

3 **A shop records how many items customers purchase from their store. The data is shown below:**

25 points

3   4   1   8   5   10   2   1   5   2   4

Create a box-and-whisker plot of the above data.

4 **Logan interviews his friends and records their age and shoe size. The data is shown below:**

20 points

Age	Shoe Size
11	7
9	5
12	7
10	7
11	8
8	4
9	4
13	9
7	4
8	6

Create a scatterplot based on Logan's data.

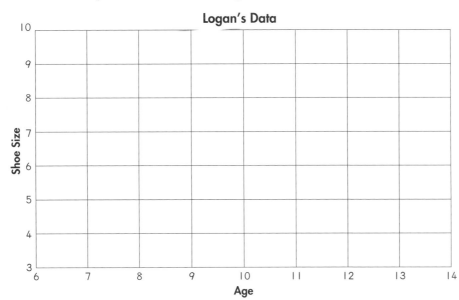

Memo

Kumon Math Workbooks

Grades **7** & **8**

Are You Ready for High School Math?

Review

Table of Contents

1 **Evaluate the following expressions:**   7 points each

(1) $10 - (-6) \div (-2) \times 3 - 1$

=

(2) $\frac{3}{4} - 2\frac{1}{2} + \left(-\frac{1}{2}\right) \div \left(-\frac{3}{5}\right)$

=

(3) $\left(-1\frac{1}{2}\right)^4 \div \left(-\frac{3}{4}\right)^3 \times \left(1\frac{1}{8}\right)$

=

(4) $(1.5) \div \left(-\frac{1}{2}\right)^3 + 2 \times (-3) - (-0.5)$

=

(5) $(-2)^5 \times [(0.25)^2 \div (-3)^2] - 1 + 5 =$

(6) $\left(-\frac{1}{2}\right)^3 \times (-5) \div \frac{1}{3} \times \left(-\frac{4}{9}\right)^2 \div \left(-\frac{5}{3}\right)^3 =$

2 **Solve each of the following equations for x.**

8 points each

(1) $5x = 3(2x + 1)$

(2) $-(2x + 9) = 3(4x - 1) + 1$

(3) $2\left(-\dfrac{3}{4}x - \dfrac{1}{2}\right) - 2x = -\left(-\dfrac{1}{3} + x\right)$

(4) $-\dfrac{6x - 7}{5} + 3 = \dfrac{4 - 3x}{2}$

3 **Solve each of the following simultaneous equations.**

13 points each

(1)

$$\begin{cases} 3x + 4y = 20 \\ -2x - 5y = -18 \end{cases}$$

(2)

$$\begin{cases} -x + 5y = -8 \\ -7x - 3y = 20 \end{cases}$$

1 You are given the shape at the right.
Use the figure to answer each of the following questions.

7 points each

(1) Find the volume of the solid.

⟨Ans.⟩ _____

(2) Find the surface area of the solid.

⟨Ans.⟩ _____

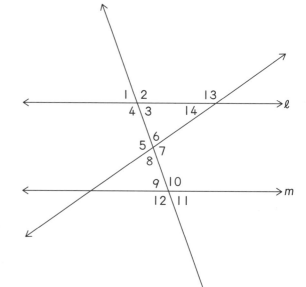

2 cm
9 cm
4 cm
7 cm
13 cm

2 You are given the shape at the right. Given that line ℓ is perpendicular to line *m*, and $m\angle 1 = 70°$ and $m\angle 13 = 145°$, answer each of the following questions.

7 points each

(1) Which angles are congruent to ∠1?

⟨Ans.⟩ _____

(2) What is the measurement of ∠14?

⟨Ans.⟩ _____

(3) What is the measurement of ∠6?

⟨Ans.⟩ _____

(4) Are the two triangles in the figure similar?

⟨Ans.⟩ _____

© Kumon Publishing Co., Ltd.

3 **Given the figure on the right, and that *ABCD* and *CEFG* are both squares. Complete the steps to prove that $\overline{BG} \cong \overline{DE}$.**   8 points each

(1) Step 1: Given *ABCD* is a square, therefore $\overline{BC} \cong$ _____
and $m\angle BCD = \boxed{}°$.

(2) Step 2: Given *CEFG* is a square, therefore $\overline{CG} \cong$ _____
and $m\angle GCE = \boxed{}°$.

(3) Step 3: Using the _____ Method,
_____ $\cong$ _____.

(4) Step 4: Given $\triangle BCG \cong \triangle DCE$, therefore
_____ $\cong$ _____.

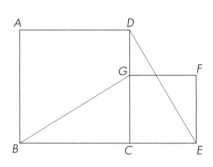

4 **Given the nets below, answer each of the following questions.**   8 points each

A   B 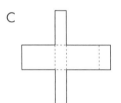 C 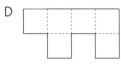 D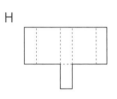

E 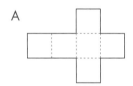 F 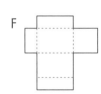 G  H

(1) Which of the nets build rectangular prisms?   〈Ans.〉 _____

(2) Which of the nets build cubes?   〈Ans.〉 _____

5 **Which of the shapes below have line symmetry?**   10 points

A Rectangle   B Rhombus   C Isosceles triangle

D Equilateral triangle   E Right triangle   F Regular pentagon

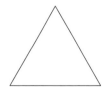 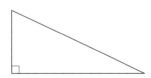

〈Ans.〉 _____

Name

Date   /   /   Score   / 100

1 Zelda counts the number of birds that fly past her window each morning for 15 days. The data is shown below:

8 points each

5   7   10   18   6   9   4   11   8   6   3   10   6   4   12

(1)   Create a histogram to represent Zelda's data.

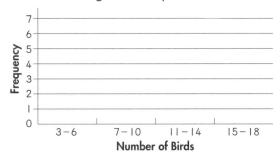

(2)   Create a box-and-whisker plot to represent Zelda's data.

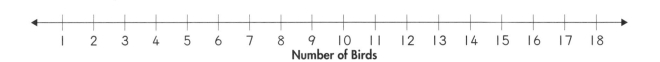

2 Rob randomly draws 1 card from a standard deck of playing cards. A standard deck of playing cards contains 52 cards, where each card has 3 identifying features: suit, color, and number (or face).

8 points each

- The 4 suits are: spades (black), hearts (red), clubs (black), and diamonds (red).
- The number cards are 2, 3, 4, 5, 6, 7, 8, 9, and 10.
- The face cards are jack, queen, and king.
- The ace card does not have a number nor a face.
- Each suit includes the 9 number cards, 3 face cards, and 1 ace card.

Use this information to answer each of the following questions.

(1)   What is the probability that Rob picks a card that does not have a number on it?

⟨**Ans.**⟩

(2)   What is the probability that Rob picks a card that is either red-colored or even?

⟨**Ans.**⟩

(3)   What is the probability that Rob picks a card that is both a spade and a face card?

⟨**Ans.**⟩

© Kumon Publishing Co., Ltd.

3 **Professor Gonzalez goes to a forest and studies monkeys by recording their color (red or white) and their size (large or small). The data is shown below:**   10 points each

	Red	White
Small	10	22
Large	12	6

Use this information to answer each of the following questions.

（1） What is the probability that Professor Gonzalez sees a large, red monkey?

〈Ans.〉 _____

（2） What is the probability that Professor Gonzalez sees a small monkey?

〈Ans.〉 _____

（3） What is the probability that Professor Gonzalez sees a monkey that is not a small, red monkey?

〈Ans.〉 _____

4 **Andy owns an ice cream shop. He keeps track of the temperature outside during lunchtime (in degrees Fahrenheit) and how many customers come into his shop during lunchtime each day. His records are shown below:**   15 points each

Temperature (°F)	Customers
74	5
85	12
68	4
67	3
73	8
78	11
81	14
76	12
82	11
71	6

（1） Create a scatterplot based on Andy's data.

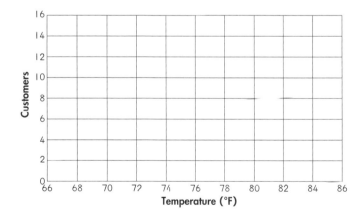

（2） What type of correlation does the data have?

〈Ans.〉 _____

Final Review 1

Name

Date ___/___/___   Score ___/100

1 What is the sum of all the interior angles for each of the following polygons?

10 points each

(1) Octagon

(a) 900° (b) 1,080° (c) 1,260° (d) 1,440°

(2) Hexagon

(a) 360° (b) 540° (c) 720° (d) 900°

(3) Decagon

(a) 720° (b) 900° (c) 1,440° (d) 1,800°

2 In the figure below, $\triangle ABC \sim \triangle A'B'C'$, where the midpoints of $\overline{BC}$ and $\overline{B'C'}$ are M and M', respectively. Show that $\triangle ABM \sim \triangle A'B'M'$ by completing each of the following steps.

7 points each

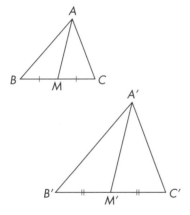

(1) Step 1: Since $\triangle ABC \sim \triangle A'B'C'$ therefore $\angle B \cong$ _____.

(2) Step 2: Since $\triangle ABC \sim \triangle A'B'C'$ therefore $\overline{AB} : \overline{A'B'} = \overline{BC} :$ _____.

(3) Step 3: Since M is the midpoint of $\overline{BC}$ and M' is the midpoint of $\overline{B'C'}$,

therefore $\overline{BC} = 2 \times$ _____ and $\overline{B'C'} = 2 \times$ _____.

(4) Step 4: Using Steps 2 and 3 : $\overline{AB} : \overline{A'B'} = 2 \times$ _____ : $2 \times$ _____.

In other words, the ratio can be expressed as: $\overline{AB} : \overline{A'B'} =$ _____ : _____.

(5) Step 5: Since $\angle B \cong$ _____ and $\overline{AB} : \overline{A'B'} =$ _____ : _____,

therefore _____.

 © Kumon Publishing Co., Ltd.

3 Simplify each of the following algebraic expressions.

5 points each

(1) $-2(3-5y)+6(-2y+3)$

=

(2) $(-a+b)-4\left(\dfrac{3}{2}a-2b\right)$

=

(3) $-\dfrac{11x-4}{6}+\dfrac{3x+8}{6}=$

(4) $\dfrac{3x-7}{4}-\dfrac{2x-5}{3}=$

4 Identify which line is the most accurate line of best fit for the scatterplot.

15 points

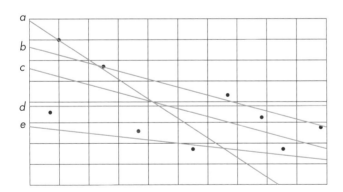

(a) a

(b) b

(c) c

(d) d

(e) e

© *Kumon Publishing Co., Ltd.*

Final Review 2

Name

Date   /   /   Score   / 100

1 Evaluate each of the following expressions.   *7 points each*

(1) $3x^2 - 2x - 8$; when $x = -\dfrac{4}{3}$

(2) $(3x + 4)(x - 2)$; when $x = -\dfrac{4}{3}$

(3) $(b^2 - c^2) - (a^2 - c^2)$; when $a = -1$, $b = 2$, and $c = -\dfrac{1}{2}$

(4) $\dfrac{a^2 b}{c} - \dfrac{b}{cd}$; when $a = -1$, $b = 2$, $c = -\dfrac{1}{4}$, and $d = -2$

2 For each of the following triangles, find the missing value.   *7 points each*

(1) Given $\triangle ABC$, where $m\angle A = 30°$, $m\angle C = 90°$, and $\overline{AB} = 5$ in., what is the length of $\overline{AC}$?

⟨**Ans.**⟩ _____

(2) Given $\triangle DEF$, where $m\angle D = 45°$, $m\angle F = 90°$, and $\overline{DE} = 8$ cm, what is the length of $\overline{EF}$?

⟨**Ans.**⟩ _____

(3) Given $\triangle GHI$, where $m\angle H = 90°$, $\overline{GH} = 2$ ft., and $\overline{GI} = 4$ ft., what is the length of $\overline{HI}$?

⟨**Ans.**⟩ _____

(4) Given $\triangle JKL$, where $m\angle J = 90°$, $\overline{JK} = 1.5$ m, and $\overline{KL} = 3$ m, what is the measurement of $\angle K$?

⟨**Ans.**⟩ _____

 © Kumon Publishing Co., Ltd.

pp. 1–65
Algebra

pp. 67–151
Geometry

pp. 153–183
Probability & Statistics

pp. 185–197
Review

3 **Which of the following statements are always correct? Choose all correct answers.**   12 points

(a) All rectangles are squares.

(b) All squares are rectangles.

(c) All rhombuses are squares.

(d) All squares are rhombuses.

(e) All parallelograms are rectangles.

(f) All rectangles are parallelograms.

4 **A standard deck of playing cards contains 52 cards, where each card has 3 identifying features: suit, color, and number (or face).**   8 points each

- The 4 suits are: spades (black), hearts (red), clubs (black), and diamonds (red).
- The number cards are 2, 3, 4, 5, 6, 7, 8, 9, and 10.
- The face cards are jack, queen, and king.
- The ace card does not have a number nor a face.
- Each suit includes the 9 number cards, 3 face cards, and 1 ace card.

Use this information to answer each of the following questions.

(1) Judith randomly draws 1 card from the deck. Determine the probability that the card shows spades.

⟨Ans.⟩ _____

(2) Rashad puts Judith's card back into the deck and shuffles the deck. He then randomly draws 1 card from the deck. Determine the probability that it is <u>not</u> a number card.

⟨Ans.⟩ _____

(3) Ling puts Rashad's card back into the deck and shuffles the deck. He then randomly draws 1 card from the deck. Determine the probability that the card is a king or is red.

⟨Ans.⟩ _____

(4) Jasmine puts Ling's card back into the deck and shuffles the deck. She then randomly draws 1 card from the deck, records what suit it is, and puts the card back into the deck, before shuffling the deck again. She then randomly draws 1 card from the deck again and records what suit it is. Determine the probability that both cards show hearts.

⟨Ans.⟩ _____

Final Review 3

Name _____

Date ____ / ____ / ____   Score _____ / 100

1 **Find the equation of each of the following lines.**   5 points each

(1) The line that is parallel to $6x + 2y = 1$ and passes through $(-1, 5)$.

⟨Ans.⟩ _____

(2) The line that is perpendicular to $x = 2y - 5$ and passes through $(3, -1)$.

⟨Ans.⟩ _____

(3) The line that is parallel to $-2x = \dfrac{3}{5} - \dfrac{1}{4}y$ and passes through $\left(-\dfrac{1}{2}, -7\right)$.

⟨Ans.⟩ _____

(4) The line that is perpendicular to $\dfrac{2}{3}x + 6y = -7$ and passes through $\left(-\dfrac{2}{3}, -\dfrac{3}{2}\right)$.

⟨Ans.⟩ _____

2 **A line passes through the points $(-1, 3)$ and $(-5, 0)$. Find the equation of the line.**   8 points each

⟨Ans.⟩ _____

3 **Select all the correct answers which satisfy each of the following conditions.**   8 points each

(1) Which shapes have diagonals that always intersect perpendicularly?

　(a) Quadrilaterals　(b) Parallelograms　(c) Rectangles　(d) Squares　(e) Rhombuses

(2) Which of the following categories do <u>all</u> rectangles belong to?

　(a) Quadrilaterals　(b) Parallelograms　(c) Squares　(d) Rhombuses　(e) Trapezoids

(3) Which of the following shapes <u>always</u> have two pairs of parallel sides?

　(a) Quadrilaterals　(b) Parallelograms　(c) Rectangles　(d) Squares　(e) Rhombuses

　© *Kumon Publishing Co., Ltd.*

pp. 1–65
Algebra

pp. 67–151
Geometry

pp. 153–183
Probability & Statistics

pp. 185–197
Review

4 **Graph each of the following equations on the coordinate plane below.** 8 points each

(a) $4x + 6y = 2$

(b) $x = -2$

(c) $y = -\dfrac{7}{2}$

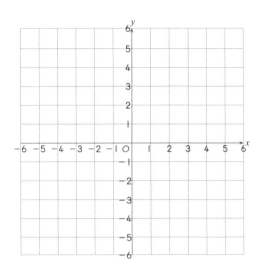

5 **A forest contains brown bears and black bears. Dr. Lee decides to record how many bears of each color she sees. There are 600 bears in the forest. Dr. Lee repeats her observations for a total of 4 times, where the results are shown below:** 8 points each

	Brown Bears	Black Bears
Experiment #1	8	4
Experiment #2	6	6
Experiment #3	9	3
Experiment #4	7	5

Use this information to answer each of the following questions.

(1) What is the average number of brown bears that Dr. Lee sees?

〈**Ans.**〉 _____

(2) What is the estimated number of black bears in the forest?

〈**Ans.**〉 _____

(3) If Dr. Lee sees a bear, is it likely that it is a brown bear or is it not likely that it is a brown bear?

〈**Ans.**〉 _____

Are You Ready for High School Math?

Answer Key

1 Fractions 1
Adding and Subtracting Fractions (pp. 2–3)

1 (1) GCF: 2, LCM: 36
(2) GCF: 1, LCM: 77
(3) GCF: 14, LCM: 42
(4) GCF: 8, LCM: 48

2 (1) $\dfrac{13}{24}$ (2) $\dfrac{5}{8}$
(3) $1\dfrac{7}{24}$ (4) $2\dfrac{1}{18}$
(5) $2\dfrac{9}{20}$ (6) $4\dfrac{17}{20}$
(7) $1\dfrac{5}{12}$ (8) $4\dfrac{7}{12}$

2 Fractions 2
Multiplying and Dividing Fractions (pp. 4–5)

1 (1) $\dfrac{8}{15}$ (2) $\dfrac{5}{12}$
(3) $1\dfrac{5}{7}$ (4) $25\dfrac{1}{2}$
(5) $1\dfrac{1}{4}$ (6) $\dfrac{14}{27}$
(7) 49   (8) $31\dfrac{1}{2}$

2 (1) $2\dfrac{1}{2} \times 6 = 15$ miles
(2) $\dfrac{2}{3} \div 2 = \dfrac{1}{3}$ pound of flour

3 Decimals and Percent (pp. 6–7)

1 (1) Fraction: $\dfrac{2}{5}$, Percent: 40 %
(2) Decimal: 0.7, Fraction: $\dfrac{7}{10}$
(3) Decimal: 1.4, Percent: 140 %

2 (1) $\dfrac{3}{5}$ (2) $3\dfrac{7}{20}$
(3) 1   (4) $4\dfrac{11}{16}$

3 $7\dfrac{1}{2} \times 3.2 \div 1.5 = 16$ pieces of paper

4 Exponents (pp. 8–9)

1 (1) 81   (2) $\dfrac{8}{27}$
(3) $5\dfrac{4}{9}$ (4) 3
(5) 16   (6) $44\dfrac{4}{9}$
(7) $\dfrac{1}{2}$ (8) $\dfrac{1}{3}$

Quiz Algebra Quiz 1 (pp. 10–11)

1 (1) $5\dfrac{19}{24}$ (2) $1\dfrac{31}{36}$
(3) $\dfrac{19}{30}$ (4) $6\dfrac{13}{28}$
(5) 24   (6) 4
(7) $3\dfrac{1}{3}$ (8) $3\dfrac{63}{64}$
(9) 5   (10) $6\dfrac{1}{2}$

2 (1) 324   (2) 100
(3) 6   (4) $1\dfrac{7}{9}$

3 (1) (b)
$4\dfrac{2}{3} \div 2 = 2\dfrac{1}{3}$
(2) (d)
$3.6 \times \dfrac{2}{3} + 1\dfrac{1}{2} = 3\dfrac{9}{10} = 3.9$

 © Kumon Publishing Co., Ltd.

5 Order of Operations 1 (pp. 12–13)

1 (1) 12 (2) 20

(3) 13 (4) $4\frac{1}{2}$

(5) 3 (6) 44

(7) $10\frac{1}{2}$ (8) $\frac{3}{50}$

2 $5 + (4^3 - 16) \times 2 = 101$ toys

6 Order of Operations 2 (pp. 14–15)

1 (1) 40 (2) 8

(3) 32 (4) 32

(5) $\frac{1}{9}$ (6) $13\frac{3}{8}$

2 (1) $(2.5 + 0.25) \times 8 = 22$ hours

(2) $\left(0.8 \times 3 + 1\frac{1}{2}\right) \times 4 = 15\frac{3}{5}$ pounds

7 Negative Numbers 1 (pp. 16–17)

1 (1) -4 (2) 22

(3) $-1\frac{11}{12}$ (4) $-4\frac{1}{12}$

2 (1) 6 (2) -120

(3) $-6\frac{2}{5}$ (4) $8\frac{3}{4}$

8 Negative Numbers 2 (pp. 18–19)

1 (1) $\frac{3}{4}$ (2) $-\frac{8}{15}$

(3) $-\frac{5}{14}$ (4) $-\frac{32}{155}$

(5) $\frac{1}{3}$ (6) $-2\frac{2}{5}$

2 $-2.5 - 1\frac{1}{4} \times 4 + 3 \times 2 = -1.5$ degrees Celsius

9 Values of Algebraic Expressions (pp. 20–21)

1 (1) -81 (2) 28

2 (1) $-\frac{7}{8}$ (2) $1\frac{3}{4}$

3 (1) $-2\frac{1}{4}$ (2) $-2\frac{1}{4}$

4 $\frac{3}{10}$

Quiz Algebra Quiz 2 (pp. 22–23)

1 (1) $\frac{5}{24}$ (2) 8

(3) 3 (4) $\frac{3}{16}$

(5) $\frac{1}{15}$ (6) $12\frac{3}{20}$

(7) -4 (8) $-2\frac{1}{2}$

2 (1) (b) (2) (c)

(3) (c) (4) (a)

3 (1) $\frac{3}{4}x$ pizzas

(2) $7\frac{1}{2}$ pizzas

10 Simplifying Algebraic Expressions 1 (pp. 24–25)

1 (1) $15b$

(2) $9a^2 + \dfrac{5}{2}ab$

(3) $-\dfrac{13}{12}x + \dfrac{5}{2}y$

(4) $-x^2 + \dfrac{5}{4}xy$

(5) $\dfrac{15}{2}k^2 + \dfrac{1}{12}m - 9$

(6) $-\dfrac{9}{2}ab - \dfrac{5}{4}bc + \dfrac{25}{3}cd$

(7) $-abc + \dfrac{5}{3}bd$

(8) $-s^2 - \dfrac{19}{12}st + t^2$

11 Simplifying Algebraic Expressions 2 (pp. 26–27)

1 (1) $5x + 5y$

(2) $10a - 7b - c$

(3) $-k + m$

(4) $\dfrac{11}{2}p^2 - \dfrac{19}{4}q$

(5) $-17x + 5y + z$

(6) $\dfrac{19}{4}a^2 - \dfrac{3}{2}ab - \dfrac{8}{5}b^2$

12 Simplifying Algebraic Expressions 3 (pp. 28–29)

1 (1) $xy + xz$　　(2) $6x - 8y$

(3) $9x + 15y$　　(4) $6x + 20$

(5) $14a + 3b$　　(6) $-7a + 15b$

(7) $-\dfrac{10}{3}x^2 - 13y^2$　(8) $-5a - \dfrac{22}{3}b - c$

13 Solving Equations 1 (pp. 30–31)

1 (1) $x = 6$　　　　(2) $x = 13$

(3) $x = -6$　　　(4) $x = -18$

(5) $x = -\dfrac{3}{2}$　　(6) $x = -12$

(7) $x = -\dfrac{7}{3}$　　(8) $x = -\dfrac{45}{8}$

14 Solving Equations 2 (pp. 32–33)

1 (1) $x = 1$　　　(2) $x = -2$

(3) $x = -\dfrac{6}{5}$　　(4) $x = -6$

(5) $x = -\dfrac{2}{39}$　　(6) $x = -\dfrac{16}{5}$

(7) $x = \dfrac{1}{6}$　　　(8) $x = 8$

15 Solving Equations 3 (pp. 34–35)

1 (1) $2x + 5 = 19; x = 7$

(2) $x \div 4 = \dfrac{3}{2}; x = 6$

2 (1) $8x = 96; 12$ pounds

(2) $8 \times 3 + 2x = 46; 11$ erasers

(3) $x + (x - 5) = 39; 22$ apples

Quiz Algebra Quiz 3 (pp. 36–37)

1 (1) (d)　　　(2) (a)

2 (1) $x = -2$　　(2) $x = -8$

(3) $x = \dfrac{16}{3}$　　(4) $x = -\dfrac{3}{2}$

3 (1) $4x = 68$; There are 17 t-shirts in the crate.

(2) $x + (x - 8) = 32$; There are 20 girls in the class.

(3) $(x + 15) = 4x$; Mike's current age is 5 years old.

(4) $2(7 + x) = 20 + x$; In 6 years, Arthur will be twice as old as Sue.

16 Simultaneous Linear Equations 1 (pp. 38–39)

1 (1) $(x, y) = (1, 3)$

(2) $(x, y) = (-2, 3)$

(3) $(x, y) = (1, 4)$

(4) $(x, y) = (-2, -5)$

(5) $(x, y) = \left(\dfrac{1}{2}, 4\right)$

(6) $(x, y) = (-2, -2)$

17 Simultaneous Linear Equations 2 (pp. 40–41)

1 (1) $(x, y) = (-3, 1)$

(2) $(x, y) = (-2, -3)$

(3) $(x, y) = \left(-\dfrac{1}{2}, 5\right)$

(4) $(x, y) = \left(-\dfrac{1}{4}, \dfrac{1}{3}\right)$

(5) $(x, y) = (-31, 52)$

(6) $(x, y) = (2, -6)$

18 Simultaneous Linear Equations 3 (pp. 42–43)

1 (1) $(x, y) = (5, -2)$

(2) $(x, y) = \left(\dfrac{1}{2}, 6\right)$

2 (1) $(x, y) = (4, -1)$

(2) $(x, y) = (4, -1)$

3 (1) $(x, y) = \left(\dfrac{1}{2}, -\dfrac{3}{2}\right)$

(2) $(x, y) = \left(\dfrac{1}{2}, -\dfrac{3}{2}\right)$

19 Inequalities (pp. 44–45)

1 (1) $x > 6$ (2) $x \geq -3$

(3) $x \geq -\dfrac{17}{3}$ (4) $x \leq \dfrac{5}{4}$

(5) $x < -5$ (6) $x \leq 9$

2 (1) $x + 8 < 5x$; $x > 2$

(2) $3(2x - 5) > \dfrac{1}{2}(-3x + 5)$; $x > \dfrac{7}{3}$

20 Ratios, Equations, and Inequalities (pp. 46–47)

1 (1) $7:9, \dfrac{7}{9}$ (2) $7:2, \dfrac{7}{2}$

2 $\dfrac{x}{60} \leq \dfrac{1}{12} \rightarrow x \leq 5$; There are 5 chefs or fewer.

3 $\dfrac{x}{200} > \dfrac{3}{8} \rightarrow x > 75$; There are more than 75 birds.

4 $\dfrac{x}{12} = \dfrac{3}{2} \rightarrow x = 18$; Sam is 18 years old.

Quiz Algebra Quiz 4 (pp. 48–49)

1 (1) $(x, y) = \left(-\dfrac{3}{4}, -1\right)$

(2) $(x, y) = \left(-\dfrac{3}{4}, -1\right)$

2 (1) $(x, y) = (3, -5)$

(2) $(x, y) = (3, -5)$

3 (1) (b) (2) (a)

4 $\dfrac{x}{28} < \dfrac{3}{4} \rightarrow x < 21$; There are fewer than 21 adults on the subway.

5 $\dfrac{x}{45} > \dfrac{3}{5} \rightarrow x > 27$; Elliot is older than 27 years old.

21 Graphs 1 (pp. 50–51)

1 (1) Point A : $(3, 7)$
(2) Point B : $(-7, -2)$
(3) Point C : $(-3, 3)$
(4) Point D : $(0, -7)$
(5) Point E : $(4, -4)$
(6) Point F : $(6, 0)$

2
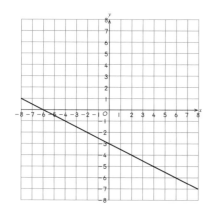

3

x	-3	-2	-1	0	1	2	3
y	$-\dfrac{3}{2}$	-2	$-\dfrac{5}{2}$	-3	$-\dfrac{7}{2}$	-4	$-\dfrac{9}{2}$

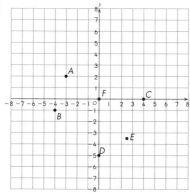

22 Graphs 2 (pp. 52–53)

1 (1) y-intercept: 3
Slope: 1
Equation: $y = x + 3$
(2) y-intercept: 1
Slope: $-\dfrac{2}{3}$
Equation: $y = -\dfrac{2}{3}x + 1$

2
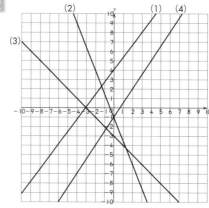

23 Functions (pp. 54–55)

1 (1) F　　　　　　(2) N
(3) F　　　　　　(4) F
(5) The graph will be a horizontal line at $y = 3$.

2 (1) Domain: {1, 2, 3, 4, 5}
Range: {6, 7, 8, 9, 10}
(2) Domain: {6, 7, 8, 9, 10}
Range: {−1, 0, 1, 2, 3}
(3) Domain: {−2, −1, 0, 1, 2}
Range: {−6, −3, 0, 3, 6}

24 Linear Functions 1 (pp. 56–57)

1 (1) 6　　　　　　(2) 4
(3) Decrease　　　(4) 2
(5) $\dfrac{2}{3}$　　　　　(6) $-\dfrac{2}{3}$
(7) $y = -\dfrac{2}{3}x + 4$

 © *Kumon Publishing Co., Ltd.*

2 (1) y-intercept: 1 (2) Slope: $\dfrac{3}{2}$

3 (1) $y = -\dfrac{3}{4}x - 2$

(2)

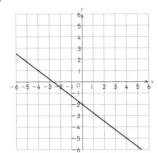

---

25 **Linear Functions 2** (pp. 58–59)

1 (1) $m = \dfrac{2}{7}$ (2) $m = -1$

2 (1) $y = -\dfrac{1}{3}x + \dfrac{5}{3}$ (2) $y = \dfrac{5}{3}x + \dfrac{1}{3}$

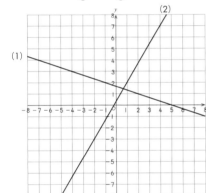

3 (1)

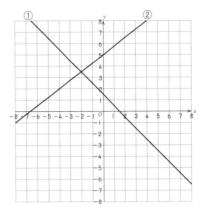

Intersection point: $\left(-2, \dfrac{7}{2}\right)$

(2) Rewrite ① as: $2y = -2x + 3$; $y = -x + \dfrac{3}{2}$.
Substitute ① into ②

→ ② becomes $3x - 4\left(-x + \dfrac{3}{2}\right) = -20$.

$$3x + 4x - 6 = -20$$
$$7x = -14$$
$$x = -2 \text{ and } y = \dfrac{7}{2}$$

Intersection point: $\left(-2, \dfrac{7}{2}\right)$

---

26 **Lines 1** (pp. 60–61)

1

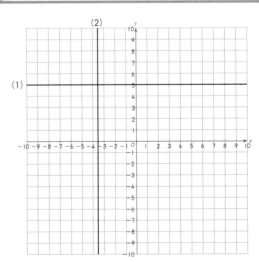

2

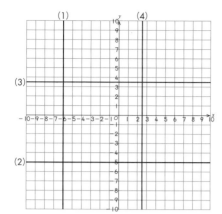

27 Lines 2

(pp. 62–63)

1 (1) $y = \dfrac{3}{4}x + 3$ or $3x - 4y = -12$

(2)

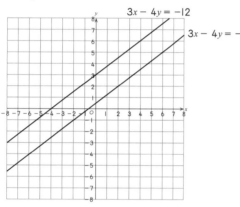

2 (1) $y = \dfrac{1}{2}x + \dfrac{13}{2}$ or $x - 2y = -13$

(2)

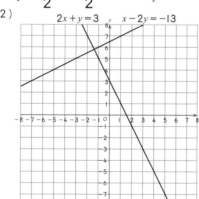

Quiz **Algebra Quiz 5** (pp. 64–65)

1

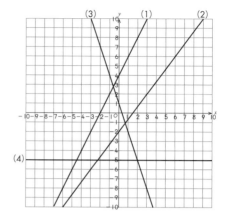

2

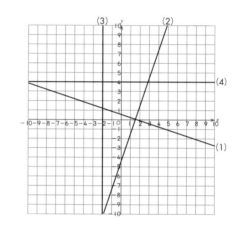

3 (1) Domain: {1, 2, 3, 4, 5}
Range: {2, 4, 6, 8, 10}
(2) Domain: {8, 9, 10, 11, 12}
Range: {−1, 0, 1, 2, 3}

4 (b)

5 (c)

28 Geometric Notation 1

(pp. 68–69)

1

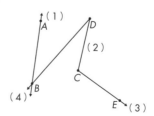

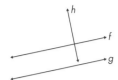

29 Geometric Notation 2
Angles and Triangles
(pp. 70–71)

1 (1) $\angle HLK \cong \angle ILJ$

(2) $\overline{IJ} \cong \overline{HK}$

(3) $\overline{KL} \cong \overline{LI}$

(4) $\angle IJK \cong \angle KHI$

(5) $\angle LKH + \angle LHI + \angle LIJ + \angle LJK = 180°$

(6) $\overline{HI} \cong \overline{KJ}$

(7) There are a total of **8 triangles**: $\triangle LHK$, $\triangle ILH$, $\triangle ILJ$, $\triangle JLK$, $\triangle HJK$, $\triangle IKH$, $\triangle JHI$, and $\triangle KIJ$.

30 Geometry Basics 1
(pp. 72–73)

1 (1) Rectangle, Square

(2) Trapezoid

(3) Parallelogram, Rhombus, Rectangle, Square

2 (1) Equilateral triangle, Isosceles triangle

(2) Isosceles triangle, Right triangle

31 Geometric Basics 2
Angles
(pp. 74–75)

1 (1) $\angle R$

(2) **$\angle P$ and $\angle Q$** are supplementary angles.
   $\angle P$ and $\angle S$ are also supplementary angles.

(3) $180°$

2 (1) $\angle 4$, $\angle 5$, $\angle 8$

(2) $\angle 3$, $\angle 6$, $\angle 7$

32 Geometric Basics 3
Perimeter, Area, and Volume
(pp. 76–77)

1 $(84 - 24) = 60 \text{ m}^2$

2 64 cm^3

3 (1) 64 cm

(2) $(2 \times 4 \times 7) = 56 \text{ cm}^3$

33 Line Symmetry and Rotational Symmetry
(pp. 78–79)

1 (1)

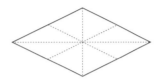

(2) (a), (b), (c)

(3)

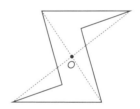

34 Circles 1
Circumference and Area
(pp. 80–81)

1 (1) $2\pi r = 2\pi \times 6 = 12\pi \text{ m}$

(2) $\pi r^2 = \pi \times (6)^2 = 36\pi \text{ m}^2$

2 (1) $(30 + 6\pi) \text{ in.}$

(2) $(90 + 9\pi) \text{ in.}^2$

3 (1) $(36 + 6\pi) \text{ ft.}$

(2) $(144 - 18\pi) \text{ ft.}^2$

35 Circles 2
Arc and Sector

1 (1) $2\pi \times 4 \times \dfrac{180}{360} = 4\pi$ in.

(2) $2 \times 4 + 4\pi = (8 + 4\pi)$ in.

(3) $\pi \times (4)^2 \times \dfrac{180}{360} = 8\pi$ in.^{2}

2 (1) $2\pi \times 6 \times \dfrac{150}{360} = 5\pi$ m

(2) $2 \times 6 + 5\pi = (12 + 5\pi)$ m

(3) $\pi \times (6)^2 \times \dfrac{150}{360} = 15\pi$ m^2

36 Construction

1

2

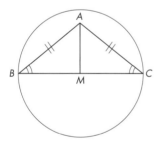

3

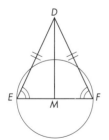

Quiz Geometry Quiz 1

1 Perimeter: $\left(10 + \dfrac{15}{2}\pi\right)$ cm

Area: $\left(25 + \dfrac{75}{4}\pi\right)$ cm^2

2 (1) (b)

(2) (e)

(3) (d)

(4) (b), (d), and (e)

3

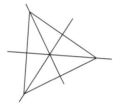

4 (1) 6π in.

(2) 9π in.^{2}

(3) π in.

(4) $(6 + \pi)$ in.

(5) $\dfrac{9}{6}\pi = \dfrac{3}{2}\pi$ in.^{2}

37 Lines, Planes, and Distance in Space

1 (1) 10 in.

(2) 2 in.

(3) 6 in.

2 (1) $m \parallel P$

(2) $\ell \perp n$

38 Solids and Nets 1 (pp. 90–91)

1 (1) Triangle
(2) Hexagon

2 (1) Rectangle
(2) 5
(3) Pentagon
(4) 2

3 (1) 4
(2) 1
(3) $\overline{AB}$, $\overline{DC}$, $\overline{OA}$, $\overline{OD}$
(4) $\overline{OA}$, $\overline{OD}$

39 Solids and Nets 2 (pp. 92–93)

1 (1) ABCN
(2) KNCH, GDEF, ABCN, HIJK

2 (1) ①, ②, ④, ⑥
(2) ④, ⑥
(3) ④

40 Cross-Section of a Solid (pp. 94–95)

1 (1) Square
(2) Square
(3) Rectangle

2 (1) Square
(2) Isosceles triangle

41 Projection of a Solid (pp. 96–97)

1 (1) (2) (3)

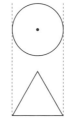 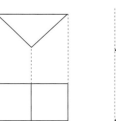

2 (1) Rectangular prism (2) Sphere

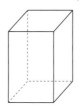

(3) Pentagonal pyramid

42 Volume and Surface Area
Solids and Spheres (pp. 98–99)

1 (1) 200π cm^3
(2) 30 in.^{3}

2 $V = \dfrac{32}{3}\pi\,\text{cm}^3$, $S = 16\pi\,\text{cm}^2$

43 Net and Surface Area
Prisms, Cylinders, Pyramids, and Cones (pp. 100–101)

1 (1) (2)

2 (1) 24, 160, 184
  (2) 25, 80, 105

3 (1)

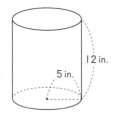

  (2) Since the area of the rectangular lateral side
      is: $12 \times (2\pi \times 5) = 120\pi$ in.^{2}, the total surface
      area is: $(25 + 25 + 120)\pi = 170\pi$ in.^{2}

Quiz Geometry Quiz 2 (pp. 102–103)

1 (1) $m \perp X$
  (2) $n \parallel Y$

2

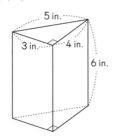

3 (1) Vertex J
  (2) Vertex B, Vertex D

4 (1)

  (2) (a)   (3) (b)   (4) (b)

44 Parallel Lines and Angles (pp. 104–105)

1 (1) F   (2) F
  (3) T   (4) F

2 (1) 35°   (2) 145°
  (3) 35°   (4) 35°
  (5) 145°
  (6) **No**, alternate angles are only congruent when
      the two lines are parallel.

45 Opposite Angle and Opposite Sides (pp. 106–107)

1 (1) **No**, $\triangle PQR$ is an obtuse triangle.
  (2) $\overline{PQ}$
  (3) Since $\angle P \cong \angle R$, their respective sides are
      also congruent. Therefore, $\overline{PR} \cong \overline{QR}$.
  (4) 35°

2 (1) 90°
  (2) 50°
  (3) Right triangle
  (4) $\overline{AC}$
  (5) $\overline{AB}$

46 Interior and Exterior Angles 1
Triangles (pp. 108–109)

1 (1) Interior angles: $\angle BCD$, $\angle CDB$, and $\angle DBC$
      Exterior angles: $\angle ABC$ and $\angle CDE$
  (2) $\angle ABC$
  (3) 180°

2 (1) 141°   (2) 90°
  (3) 129°   (4) 360°

3 65°

47 Interior and Exterior Angles 2
Polygons (pp. 110–111)

1 (1) 5   (2) 6
  (3) 8   (4) 9
  (5) 10   (6) 12

2 (1) 1,800°   (2) 1,080°

 © Kumon Publishing Co., Ltd.

3 (1) 95°   (2) 60°

48 Circles
Tangent Lines and Inscribed Angles
(pp. 112–113)

1 (1) 30°   (2) 70°
(3) Since $\overset{\frown}{AB}$ is proportional to $\angle AOB$ but is also proportional to $\angle ACB$, $m\angle x = 100°$.

2 (1) 100°   (2) 50°

3 130°

4 Since $m\angle AOB = 45°$ and $m\angle BOC = 135°$, the measurements of $\overset{\frown}{AB}$ and $\overset{\frown}{BC}$ must also be proportional.
Since 135° is three times 45°, so $\overset{\frown}{BC} = 30$ cm.

Quiz Geometry Quiz 3
(pp. 114–115)

1 (1) $m\angle x = 60°$
(2) $m\angle x = 120°$, $m\angle y = 55°$

2 (1) 145°
(2) Obtuse triangle
(3) $\overline{AC}$
(4) $\overline{BC}$

3 (1) $m\angle x = 115°$, $m\angle y = 145°$
(2) $m\angle x = 58°$
(3) $m\angle x = 85°$

4 (1) (d)
(2) (e)

49 Congruence
(pp. 116–117)

1 (1) $\triangle NQO$
(2) $\angle OPM$, $\angle PMN$, $\angle MNO$

2 (1) $\overline{CD}$
(2) $\angle g$

3 (1) $\overline{BM} \cong \overline{MC}$
(2) Side-Angle-Side (SAS)

4 (1) $\overline{AO}$, $\overline{CO}$
(2) $\overline{BO} \cong \overline{DO}$
(3) $\angle AOB \cong \angle COD$
(4) Side-Angle-Side (SAS)

50 Triangles 1
Isosceles Triangles
(pp. 118–119)

1 (1) $\angle G$ (2) $\angle H$
(3) $\angle H$ (4) isosceles

2 (1) isosceles
(2) $\angle ACB$
(3) $\angle ABD$, $\angle ACE$
(4) $\triangle ACE$
(5) $\overline{AE}$
(6) isosceles

3 (1) isosceles
(2) $\overline{AC}$
(3) $\overline{AC}$
(4) equilateral

51 Triangles 2
Equilateral Triangles
(pp. 120–121)

1 Since $\triangle ABC$ is an equilateral triangle, it is also an isosceles triangle. Therefore, $\overline{AM} \perp \overline{BC}$ and likewise $\overline{BN} \perp \overline{AC}$ and $\overline{CO} \perp \overline{AB}$.

2 (1) 6 cm   (2) 3 cm
(3) 30°

3 (1) $\overline{BC}$, $\overline{CA}$
(2) $\overline{FC}$
(3) Side-Angle-Side (SAS)
(4) $\overline{FD}$, $\overline{DE}$
(5) equilateral

52 Triangles 3
Right Triangles

1 (1) 54°   (2) 36°
(3) 54°
(4) There are **three** hypotenuses:
  • $\overline{AB}$ (hypotenuse of △ABD)
  • $\overline{BC}$ (hypotenuse of △ABC), and
  • $\overline{AC}$ (hypotenuse of △ADC)

2 (1) 45°   (2) 22.5°
(3) 112.5°   (4) 67.5°

3 (1) ∠CAD
(2) $\overline{BC}$
(3) ∠ADB ≅ ∠ADC, 90°
(4) Angle-Side-Angle (ASA)

53 Quadrilaterals 1
Parallelograms
(pp. 124–125)

1 (1) 8 in.   (2) 100°
(3) 80°   (4) 5 in.

2 (1) $\overline{ZO}$
(2) $\overline{YO}$
(3) ∠ZOY
(4) Side-Angle-Side (SAS)

54 Quadrilaterals 2
Rectangles and Squares
(pp. 126–127)

1 (1) 90
(2) $\overline{CD}$
(3) ∠CDB
(4) Angle-Side-Angle (ASA)

2 (1) 90
(2) Side-Angle-Side (SAS)
(3) $\overline{KL} \cong \overline{LM}$
(4) isosceles, 45
(5) 45
(6) 90
(7) 90
(8) square

55 Quadrilaterals 3
Rhombuses
(pp. 128–129)

1 (1) $\overline{IO}$
(2) $\overline{HO}$
(3) $\overline{HI}$
(4) Side-Side-Side (SSS)

2 (1) ∠O   (2) ∠LYO
(3) ∠OLY   (4) $\overline{LO}$
(5) Angle-Side-Angle (ASA)
(6) $\overline{OY}$

3 (1) T   (2) F
(3) T   (4) T

56 Ratios
(pp. 130–131)

1 (1) 72   (2) 6
(3) 5

2 (1) 1 : 3
(2) 2 : 8, 1 : 4
(3) $\frac{1}{2}$ × (base) × (height), 1 : 4

3 (1) 4 : 5   (2) 1 : 1
(3) 4 : 5

4 1 : 2

210   © Kumon Publishing Co., Ltd.

Quiz Geometry Quiz 4
(pp. 132–133)

1 $m\angle x = 50°$, $m\angle y = 140°$

2 (1) (b)   (2) (d)

3 (1) $\angle ABC$ (2) $\angle ACB$
(3) isosceles   (4) $\angle ACB$
(5) $\angle DCB$
(6) $\triangle EBC$ is an isosceles triangle

4 (1) rhombus
(2) rectangle
(3) square

5 (1) $\overline{CB} \cong \overline{BA}$
(2) $\angle BCD$
(3) Side-Angle-Side (SAS), $\triangle CBD$
(4) $\angle CBD$, $\angle CDB$
(5) $\overline{BD}$ bisects both $\angle ABC$ and $\angle CDA$

---

57 Transformations 1
Translation and Reflection
(pp. 134–135)

1 (1)
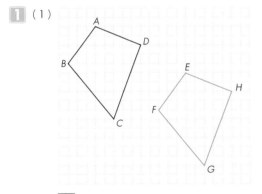

(2) $\overline{EH}$
(3) $\angle G$

2
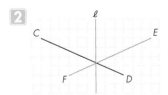

---

3 (1)
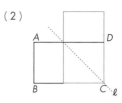
(2)
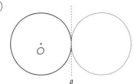

(3)

(4)

(5)
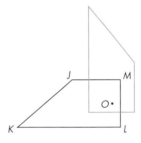

---

58 Transformations 2
Rotation, Point Symmetry, and Dilation
(pp. 136–137)

1 (1)
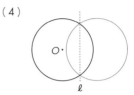

(2)
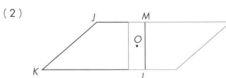

2 (1) T   (2) D
(3) Re   (4) Ro
(5) Re   (6) Ro

---

59 Similar Triangles 1
(pp. 138–139)

1 (1) 2:3   (2) 4.2 cm
(3) 12.6 cm   (4) 6 cm

2 (1) 60° (2) 90°
(3) 4 cm (4) 4.8 cm

3 (1) $\overline{OM} : \overline{RP}$ (2) $\angle PQR$
(3) $\angle MNO$, $\angle PQR$, $\angle OMN$, $\angle RPQ$

60 Similar Triangles 2
(pp. 140–141)

1 (1) 9 cm
(2) 16 cm

2 (1) 1 : 3
(2) ABC, AED

61 Area of a Square and the Pythagorean Theorem
(pp. 142–143)

1 (1) $(1.2)^2 = 1.44$
(2) square root, $2\sqrt{3}$

2 (1) 12
(2) $3\sqrt{2}$
(3) 2^2, x^2, $2\sqrt{10}$

3 (1) 9 in.² (2) $\sqrt{7}$ cm
(3) $5\sqrt{2}$ m (4) 5 m²
(5) $6\sqrt{2}$ mm (6) 12 cm²

4 (1) 10 cm (2) 15 m
(3) $\sqrt{13}$ in. (4) $\sqrt{22}$ cm
(5) $\sqrt{3}$ m (6) $\sqrt{2}$ in.

62 Special Right Triangles 1
30°–60°–90° Triangles
(pp. 144–145)

1 (1) 2 : 1, $\overline{DE} = \dfrac{5}{2} = 2.5$ in.
(2) 2 : $\sqrt{3}$, $\overline{EF} = \dfrac{5\sqrt{3}}{2}$ in.

2 (1) $3\sqrt{3}$ cm (2) 6 cm

3 (1) 16 in. (2) 8 in.

4 (1) $\dfrac{7}{\sqrt{3}} = \dfrac{7\sqrt{3}}{3}$ mm (2) $\dfrac{14\sqrt{3}}{3}$ mm

63 Special Right Triangles 2
45°–45°–90° Triangles
(pp. 146–147)

1 (1) $\sqrt{2}$: 1, $\overline{DE} = \sqrt{3}$ cm
(2) $\overline{DF} = \sqrt{3}$ cm

2 (1) $\overline{DE} = 4\sqrt{2}$ mm, $\overline{EF} = 4$ mm
(2) $\overline{GH} = 5$ m, $\overline{HI} = 5$ m
(3) $\overline{MN} = 8$ in., $\overline{LN} = 8\sqrt{2}$ in.

64 Applications of the Pythagorean Theorem
(pp. 148–149)

1 (1) Since $\triangle ABH \cong \triangle BHC \cong \triangle CHA$, therefore the area of each of these three triangles are equal. Therefore, each triangle is $\dfrac{1}{3}$ the area of $\triangle ABC$.
(2) $\dfrac{16\sqrt{3}}{3}$ cm²
(3) $\dfrac{4\sqrt{3}}{3}$ cm

2 (1) $3\sqrt{5}$
(2) $\sqrt{61}$
(3) $\sqrt{(x_2 - x_1)^2 + (y_2 - y_1)^2}$ or $\sqrt{(x_1 - x_2)^2 + (y_1 - y_2)^2}$

Quiz Geometry Quiz 5
(pp. 150–151)

1
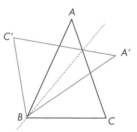

2

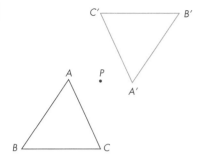

3 (1) 3 : 2
    (2) 2 cm

4 (1) $2\sqrt{3}$ in.
    (2) $2\sqrt{7}$ in.

5 (1) (d)
    (2) (b)

---

65 Theoretical Probability   (pp. 154–155)

1 (1) $\dfrac{1}{7}$

    (2) Since there is only 1 Ticket #7, the answer is: $\dfrac{1}{7}$.

    (3) 2, 4, and 6 are even numbers. Since there are 3 even number tickets, the answer is: $\dfrac{3}{7}$.

    (4) 3 and 6 are multiples of 3. Since there are 2 tickets that are a multiple of 3, the answer is: $\dfrac{2}{7}$.

    (5) 1, 2, 3, 4, and 5 are numbers from 1 to 5. Since there are 5 tickets that have a number from 1 to 5, the answer is: $\dfrac{5}{7}$.

    (6) 3, 4, 5, 6, and 7 are all greater than 2. Since there are 5 tickets that have a number greater than 2, the answer is: $\dfrac{5}{7}$.

2 (1) $\dfrac{1}{2}$
    (2) $P(\text{tails}) = \dfrac{1}{2}$

---

3 (1) $\dfrac{1}{6}$

    (2) $\dfrac{3}{6} = \dfrac{1}{2}$

    (3) $\dfrac{1}{6}$

    (4) $\dfrac{1}{6}$

---

66 Relative Frequency   (pp. 156–157)

1 (1) A $= \dfrac{57}{150} = 38\%$

    (2) B $= \dfrac{264}{500} = 52.8\%$

    (3) C $= \dfrac{343}{700} = 49\%$

    (4) D $= \dfrac{500}{1,000} = 50\%$

    (5) Ms. Smith was **correct** because as Jack performed more flips, the relative frequency reached 50%.

2 (1) A $= \dfrac{2}{16} = 12.5\%$

    (2) B $= \dfrac{12}{75} = 16\%$

    (3) C $= \dfrac{80}{250} = 32\%$

    (4) D $= \dfrac{162}{600} = 27\%$

    (5) E $= \dfrac{201}{800} = 25.125\%$

    (6) 25%

1 (1) $P(\text{bird}) = \dfrac{1}{4} = 25\%$

(2) $P(\text{green}) = \dfrac{2}{4} = 50\%$

(3) $P(\text{animal}) = \dfrac{4}{4} = 100\%$

(4) $P(\text{lion}) = \dfrac{0}{4} = 0\%$

(5) $P(\textbf{bird}) = 25\%$ is unlikely, $P(\text{lion}) = 0\%$ is impossible, $P(\text{animal}) = 100\%$ is certain, and $P(\text{green}) = 50\%$ is none of the above.

2 (1) $P(\text{J, Q, K}) = \dfrac{12}{52} = \dfrac{3}{13} \approx 23.08\%$; unlikely

(2) $P(\text{red}) = \dfrac{26}{52} = \dfrac{1}{2} = 50\%$; none of the above

(3) $P(\text{club or red}) = \dfrac{39}{52} = \dfrac{3}{4} = 75\%$; likely

(4) $P(\text{heart or black}) = \dfrac{39}{52} = \dfrac{3}{4} = 75\%$; likely

(5) $P(\text{diamond and red}) = \dfrac{13}{52} = \dfrac{1}{4} = 25\%$; unlikely

(6) $P(\text{black and even}) = \dfrac{10}{52} = \dfrac{5}{26} \approx 19.23\%$; unlikely

(7) $P(\text{black or even}) = \dfrac{36}{52} = \dfrac{9}{13} \approx 69.23\%$; likely

(8) $P(\text{black or red}) = \dfrac{52}{52} = 1 = 100\%$; certain

(9) $P(\text{diamond or heart}) = \dfrac{26}{52} = \dfrac{1}{2} = 50\%$; none of the above

(10) $P(\text{diamond and even}) = \dfrac{5}{52} \approx 9.62\%$; unlikely

1 (1) Purple

(2) $\dfrac{1}{3} \approx 33.33\%$

(3) $\dfrac{1}{3} \approx 33.33\%$

(4) $\dfrac{1}{3} \approx 33.33\%$

(5) $\dfrac{2}{3} \approx 66.67\%$

2 (1) A : T
B : H

(2) $P(\text{H}) = \dfrac{1}{2} = 50\%$

(3) $P(\text{HH}) = \dfrac{1}{2} \times \dfrac{1}{2} = \dfrac{1}{4} = 25\%$

(4) $P(\text{HT}) = \dfrac{1}{2} \times \dfrac{1}{2} = \dfrac{1}{4} = 25\%$

$P(\text{TH}) = \dfrac{1}{2} \times \dfrac{1}{2} = \dfrac{1}{4} = 25\%$

$P(\text{H and T}) = 25\% + 25\% = 50\%$

1 (1) P (2) S
(3) S (4) S
(5) P

2 (1) 2,500 students
(2) 100 students

3 (1) 7.2 orange fish; 12.8 yellow fish

(2) 36%; $\dfrac{12.8}{20} = 64\%$

(3) $36\% \times 3,000 = 1,080$ orange fish;
$64\% \times 3,000 = 1,920$ yellow fish

70 Two-Way Tables (pp. 164–165)

1 (1) $\dfrac{32}{80} = 40\%$

(2) $\dfrac{46}{80} = 57.5\%$

(3) $\dfrac{34}{80} = 42.5\%$

(4) $\dfrac{22}{32} = 68.75\%$

2 (1) 3 ; 3 ; 9

(2) 2 ; the probability is: $\dfrac{2}{9} \approx 22.22\%$

(3) $1 - \dfrac{2}{9} = \dfrac{7}{9} \approx 77.78\%$

Quiz Probability Quiz (pp. 166–167)

1 (1) $\dfrac{2}{6} = \dfrac{1}{3} \approx 33.33\%$

(2) $\dfrac{5}{6} \approx 83.33\%$

(3) Since a square, a rectangle, and a diamond each have 4 sides, the answer is: $\dfrac{3}{6} = \dfrac{1}{2}$ $= 50\%$

(4) Since the probability of $\dfrac{1}{6} \approx 16.67\%$ is closer to 0% than 50% or 100%, this event is **unlikely**.

2 (1) Using a tree diagram, the probability of selecting a blue marble both times is $\dfrac{1}{3} \times \dfrac{1}{3}$ $= \dfrac{1}{9} \approx 11.11\%$

(2) $\dfrac{1}{9} + \dfrac{1}{9} = \dfrac{2}{9} \approx 22.22\%$

3 Estimated number of gray toys: $\dfrac{4.5}{12} \times 680$ $= 255$ toys
Estimated number of purple toys: $\dfrac{7.5}{12} \times 680$ $= 425$ toys

4 (1) (d)
(2) (c)
(3) (e)

71 Frequency Distribution and Histograms (pp. 168–169)

1 A : 3
B : 6
C : 4
D : 3
E : 2

2

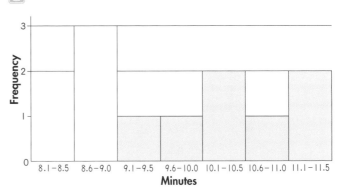

72 Maximum, Minimum, and Range (pp. 170–171)

1 (1) (80,) 72, 71, 70, 70, 68, 68, 68, 67, 65, 64, 62
(2) 80
(3) 62
(4) 18

2 (1) 70 cups of coffee
(2) 8 cups of coffee
(3) 62 cups of coffee

73 Median, Mean, and Mode (pp. 172–173)

1 (1) $\dfrac{93}{15} = 6.2$

(2) 2, 3, 3, 3, 4, 5, 6, 6, 8, 8, 8, 8, 9, 10, 10
(3) Out of the 15 amounts, the middle value is the 8th amount, which is: 6.
(4) The amount that occurs the most is: 8.

2 (1) The mean is: $\frac{45}{25} = 1.8$ pets.

(2) Out of the 25 amounts, the middle amount is the 13ᵗʰ amount, which is: 1 pet.

(3) The amount that occurs the most is: 1 pet.

74 Quartiles and IQR (pp. 174–175)

1 (1) Out of the 11 numbers, the median is the 6ᵗʰ number, which is: 7 seashells.

(2) The numbers that are below the median are: 3, 4, 5, 5, 6. Out of these 5 numbers, the median is the 3ʳᵈ number, which is: 5 seashells.

(3) The numbers that are above the median are: 8, 8, 9, 10, 11. Out of these 5 numbers, the median is the 3ʳᵈ number, which is: 9 seashells.

(4) Since Q3 is 9 seashells and Q1 is 5 seashells, therefore IQR = 9 − 5 = 4 seashells.

2 (1) Out of the 7 numbers, the median is the 4ᵗʰ number, which is: 40 minutes.

(2) Out of the 3 numbers in the lower half, Q1 is the 2ⁿᵈ number, which is: 30 minutes.

(3) Out of the 3 numbers in the upper half, Q3 is the 2ⁿᵈ number, which is: 45 minutes.

(4) Since Q3 is 45 minutes and Q1 is 30 minutes, IQR = 45 − 30 = 15 minutes.

75 Box-and-Whisker Plots (pp. 176–177)

1 (1) Minimum: 2, Q1: 4, Median: 6, Q3: 9, Maximum: 13

(2)

Points Scored

2 (1)

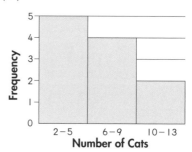

(2)

Number of Cats

76 Scatterplots (pp. 178–179)

1 (1)

(2) The more cookies that are bought, the more money will be spent.

(3) Positive correlation

2 Sample answer: Number of baby teeth (starting at 1 year old).

77 Line of Best Fit (pp. 180–181)

1 (1) Positive correlation

(2) ②

2 (1) Negative correlation

(2) ④

 © Kumon Publishing Co., Ltd.

Quiz Statistics Quiz (pp. 182-183)

1

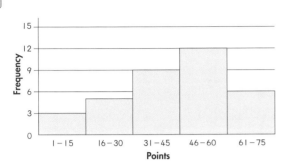

2 (1) (d)

(2) (c)

(3) (e)

3

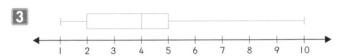

4

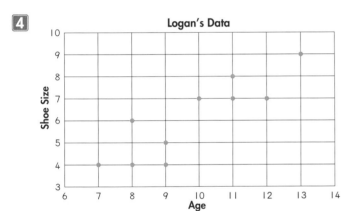

78 Algebra Review (pp. 186-187)

1 (1) 0

(2) $-\dfrac{11}{12}$

(3) $-13\dfrac{1}{2}$

(4) $-17\dfrac{1}{2}$

(5) $3\dfrac{7}{9}$

(6) $-\dfrac{2}{25}$

2 (1) $x = -3$

(2) $x = -\dfrac{1}{2}$

(3) $x = -\dfrac{8}{15}$

(4) $x = -8$

3 (1) $(4, 2)$

(2) $(-2, -2)$

79 Geometry Review (pp. 188-189)

1 (1) 434 cm^3 (2) 432 cm^2

2 (1) $\angle 3$, $\angle 9$, and $\angle 11$

(2) $m\angle 14 = 35°$

(3) $m\angle 6 = 75°$

(4) **Yes**, because the corresponding angles of the triangles are congruent.

3 (1) $\overline{BC} \cong \overline{DC}$, $\angle BCD = 90°$

(2) $\overline{CG} \cong \overline{CE}$, $\angle GCE = 90°$

(3) Side-Angle-Side (SAS), $\triangle BCG \cong \triangle DCE$

(4) $\overline{BG} \cong \overline{DE}$

4 (1) B, C

(2) A, E

5 (1) A, B, C, D, F

80 Probability & Statistics Review (pp. 190-191)

1 (1)

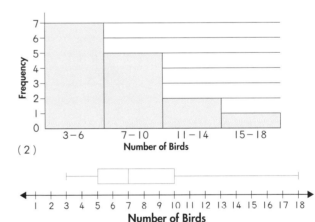

(2)

2 (1) $\dfrac{4}{13} \approx 30.77\%$

(2) $\dfrac{9}{13} \approx 69.23\%$

(3) $\dfrac{3}{52} \approx 5.77\%$

3 (1) $\dfrac{6}{25} = 24\%$

(2) $\dfrac{16}{25} = 64\%$

(3) $\dfrac{4}{5} = 80\%$

4 (1)

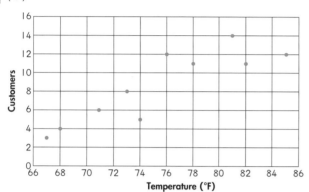

Customers vs. Temperature (°F)

(2) Positive correlation

81 Final Review 1 (pp. 192–193)

1 (1) (b)　　　(2) (c)　　　(3) (c)

2 (1) $\angle B'$
(2) $\overline{B'C'}$
(3) $\overline{BM}$, $\overline{B'M'}$
(4) $\overline{BM}$, $\overline{B'M'}$, $\overline{BM}$, $\overline{B'M'}$
(5) $\angle B'$, $\overline{BM}$, $\overline{B'M'}$, $\triangle ABM \sim \triangle A'B'M'$

3 (1) $-2y + 12$　　　(2) $-7a + 9b$
(3) $\dfrac{-4x + 6}{3}$ or $-\dfrac{4}{3}x + 2$
(4) $\dfrac{x - 1}{12}$ or $-\dfrac{x}{12} - \dfrac{1}{12}$

4 (c)

82 Final Review 2 (pp. 194–195)

1 (1) 0
(2) 0
(3) 3
(4) -12

2 (1) $\dfrac{5\sqrt{3}}{2}$ in.　　　(2) $4\sqrt{2}$ cm
(3) $2\sqrt{3}$ ft.　　　(4) $60°$

3 (b), (d), (f)

4 (1) $\dfrac{1}{4} = 25\%$
(2) $\dfrac{4}{13} \approx 30.77\%$
(3) $\dfrac{7}{13} \approx 53.85\%$
(4) $\dfrac{1}{4} \times \dfrac{1}{4} = \dfrac{1}{16} = 6.25\%$

83 Final Review 3 (pp. 196–197)

1 (1) $y = -3x + 2$
(2) $y = -2x + 5$
(3) $y = 8x - 3$
(4) $y = 9x + \dfrac{9}{2}$

2 $y = \dfrac{3}{4}x + \dfrac{15}{4}$

3 (1) (d), (e)
(2) (a), (b)
(3) (b), (c), (d), (e)

4

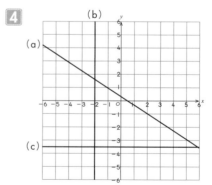

5 (1) 7.5 brown bears
(2) 225 black bears
(3) It is **likely** that it is a brown bear.

　© Kumon Publishing Co., Ltd.

Memo

Memo

Memo

Memo

Memo

Memo